why
CHRISTIAN?

Also by Douglas John Hall

Confessing the Faith:
Christian Theology in a North American Context (1996)

God and the Nations
(with Rosemary Radford Ruether, 1995)

Professing the Faith:
Christian Theology in a North American Context (1993)

Thinking the Faith:
Christian Theology in a North American Context (1989)

God and Human Suffering:
An Exercise in the Theology of the Cross (1982)

why *CHRISTIAN?*

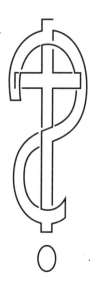

Douglas John Hall

for those on the edge of faith

Fortress Press / Minneapolis

For C. K. H.

WHY CHRISTIAN?
For Those on the Edge of Faith

Cover design: Brad Norr Design
Text design: David B. Lott

Library of Congress Cataloging-in-Publication Data

    Hall, Douglas John , 1928–
        Why Christian? : for those on the edge of faith / Douglas John
    Hall.
          p.   cm.
        Includes bibliographical references.
        ISBN 0-8006-3130-7 (alk. paper)
        1. Apologetics. I. Title.
    BT 1102.H315   1998
    239—dc21   98-10547
                                                        CIP

The paper used in this publication meets the minimum requirements of American National Standard for Information Sciences—Permanence of Paper for Printed Library Materials, ANSI Z329.48-1984.

Manufactured in the U.S.A.   AF 1-3130

02   01   00   99   98   1   2   3   4   5   6   7   8   9   10

Contents

"Faith that does not doubt is dead faith."
—MIGUEL DE UNAMUNO

"As for me, I regard myself as a Christian.
Nevertheless, I know how difficult it has been for me,
and still is, to apprehend and keep this cornerstone [Christ]."
—MARTIN LUTHER

Preface

This is a book for people on the edges—the edges of faith, the edges of the Christian tradition, in some cases the edges of the church.

In my experience, there are a great many such people in our once-Christian society. In fact, most of the people I know belong to that number in one way or another. Some of them are literally on the edges of Christian congregations, feeling themselves to be outsiders, but not quite ready to leave it all behind. Others are on the periphery of the faith spiritually and intellectually, even though they do "go to church" and are, in more than a few instances, active church members or even ministers of congregations.

Still others are one, two, or three generations removed from any specific Christian commitment. They may be the children or grandchildren of loyal churchfolk, who out of respect for their progenitors feel some lingering connections with Christianity, or are caused by present-day experiences to reconsider "religion." Many of my undergraduate students over the past thirty-five years have been in that situation. They aren't fighting Christianity, as many of my own youthful contemporaries were doing forty years ago when churches were still very much part of the authority structure of our society. Rather, many young people today are far enough away from Christianity to be curious about it again. They don't know very much about it and they doubt much of what they think they know. Still, they are well enough informed about the Christian faith to suspect that it is not being accurately represented today by the most vociferous self-declared Christians.

This book is for all of the above.

This book takes the form of dialogues between an aging professor of Christian theology (myself!) and a university undergraduate. The dialogues at the beginning of each chapter pose the question to which the rest of the chapter—the little "essays" this wonderfully conscientious professor prepares for his student—tries to respond.

The student is not identified as to name or gender or field of study. A clever reader could probably compose an interesting biography of this student from the things that are revealed about her or him, but I wanted to be as faithful as possible to the prototype. And the prototype of the person identified only as "you" is a whole professional lifetime of students—male and female, younger and older, members of nearly every faculty and discipline in the contemporary university.

In other words, the "you" is a composite—a figure of my imagination, of course, but an imagination educated by hundreds of people who as my students were also my teachers. The "you" figure also includes four young people who were never my students but are my own children. I have dedicated the book to one of them. Though I am the sole author of the lines that "you" speaks, I can assure the reader that most of those lines are paraphrases of statements made to me many times over in the course of the years.

While the person specificially addressed here is a university student, however, he or she could just as easily be a working person, a young professional, a middle-aged father or mother of adolescent children, a grandparent like myself—really, almost anybody. Anybody who lives on the edges, between faith and doubt, like one of my correspondents, who makes his living as a construction worker, and whose last letter confessed: "I've always felt drawn to God and to the hope that life has meaning. Often I struggle with—for want of a better word—nihilism. There is so much suffering and evil in the world. Belief in a good God is not an easy thing for anyone who 'thinks' to any significant degree."

It's that kind of doubting faith—or faithful doubt—with which I've wanted to dialogue here. I think I understand it. It's where I live too, most of the time.

Why Christian?

o
n
e

"I'm sorry, but I don't see why anybody today would be a Christian."

You said this calmly and, it seemed to me, with a twinge of genuine regret. I knew that the regret, in part, was because you respected me, basically. You were "sorry" because you couldn't imagine how somebody you thought both truthful and intelligent would believe "all that." But I suspected that your reluctance went deeper. Didn't it betray a certain wistfulness? Were you still harboring some hope that the Christian account of the world—or what you understood of it—might be true?

Seeing you there in the big chair in my study, the winter sun just beginning to go down, I thought of that scene in the Gospels where a young person of means and integrity came to Jesus asking how he could find "eternal life." Jesus realized that with all his possibilities—wealth, health, intelligence—the man felt incomplete, perhaps even lost. And Mark says that Jesus "looking at him, loved him . . ." (Mark 10:21). I loved you too, in that moment especially. You seemed to me to be speaking for an entire generation—in a way, for the species as a whole. How today could any honest person believe in God, let alone the God of the Christians? It's often my question, too. Don't imagine that I'm immune to its allure! Faith doesn't protect a person from such questions. In fact, faith is what it is—faith, not certitude—just

1

because it is a dialogue with the kind of doubt to which you were giving vent.

Jesus told the rich man that night long ago that the answer he was looking for lay in giving up his wealth and seeking solidarity with the poor. Maybe that is what I should have said to you, too—or something like that. But I realized that such a response, while it might in the long run be right, could not be heard by you just now. You are not, after all, Jesus' contemporary—and you certainly aren't rich! That young man of the first century may have had his misgivings, but he was obviously a believer. Not, of course, a Christian (there weren't any at that point), but a Jewish believer, who, as he insisted, had "kept all the commandments from his youth onwards." You, on the other hand, must live on the far side of Western humanity's half-decision that God, if not quite "dead," is probably only a convenient fiction.

You were conscious of my hesitation, perhaps of my complicity in your skepticism, so you pressed the question home rather mercilessly. Evidently you intended to prevent me from answering you with generalities—the sorts of generalities that come easily, after awhile, to people like me, Christian "professionals":

"Why are you a Christian?" you blurted out. "Isn't it just because you were born into a so-called Christian society? Isn't it mere habit, convention, imitation? And haven't you maybe got caught in a professional trap? Your whole vocation, not to mention your livelihood and your sense of self-worth, depends on your continuing to act out decisions that you took in your youth. . . ."

You saw me wince then, so you became a little more objective. "I mean," you went on, "why would anybody actually choose Christianity today? God knows Christian history, apart from a few exceptional people and events, is too full of horrors to persuade anybody of its superiority. As for the church today, it's pretty irrelevant to my generation—not to say plain boring. Besides, we now know very well—and not just in theory—that there are hundreds of other possibilities religiously speaking, all the way from downright atheism or a working humanism to Islam, Buddhism, or one of the other "world religions." If Christianity is just an accident of birth then it's no more convincing than any other religion that belongs to a specific geographic and historical setting. If, on the other hand, it is only a matter of personal choice, how can you avoid the charge of arbitrariness?"

I'm sure my sputtering response to this didn't impress you. The truth is, your questions challenged me to the extent that I've done something I have never done before, though I have often thought of it: I've recorded (as you can see) the gist of our conversation, and then produced a written response to your question, "Why Christian?" I confess, I did it as much for myself as for you. You made me realize that after all these years I needed to face that question in the quite basic and personal way you put it to me. I hope, though, that my "answer" will have some meaning for you. Read it over, and we'll go on from there. Maybe this can become a pattern for later discussions.

Causes and Reasons

The question, Why would anyone be Christian today? becomes more pointed when it is flung at individuals who claim that identity for themselves. I know that it will not settle all the aspects of the big historical question if I begin by responding in a personal way, but at least it will prevent me from answering your perfectly reasonable challenge as if I were addressing a public meeting! It may also help us to get to the heart of the matter.

It's quite true that, unlike you, I was born into an avowedly "Christian" culture—indeed, on the surface, it was almost monolithically so. You and I are only a generation or two apart, but in that short period of time there have been enormous changes, and nowhere are the changes more evident than in the sphere of religion. Here and there our once-Christian culture can still appear to thrive, and vestiges of it still exist everywhere—in our laws, our language, our literature. Even our curses still bear witness to Christendom, though significantly, if you've noticed, sex (especially that ubiquitous f-word) has nearly replaced religion as the main source of our expletives. Christendom hasn't disappeared altogether, but if you have lived for fifty or sixty years you know that it is by no means what it used to be.

That big social change is closely connected with the answer I must give to your question, Why Christian? In fact, your question itself—which is not just your question—is a clear pointer to the change. Few of us in my youth would ever have thought of asking it.

But let me be concrete. I grew up in a village—a great many of us North Americans lived in villages and small towns or on farms in the 1930s and 1940s. The great migration to the cities came later, and that is certainly part of the background that such a question as yours assumes. What we call "secularism," a name given to the growing agnosticism, skepticism, and atheism of Western peoples in the mid-nineteenth century, is inseparable from the industrial revolution and the gradual relocation of the population in ever-growing cities.

In the little village of my childhood and adolescence—population 307 by my own census in about 1940—nearly everybody went to church. In this case that means to a Protestant church, of which there were two, barely distinguishable from each other. There were no Roman Catholics in our area until, in the late thirties and early forties, some eastern European immigrants began to take over the "poorer" agricultural properties of the district and turn them into goldmines as tobacco farms. (Incidentally, tobacco having meanwhile amply documented its wicked ways, today the same farms are being transformed into new goldmines by growing the Asiatic product ginseng, indicating yet another population shift.) Buddhists, Muslims, Confucianists, and others of whom we knew, a few of us, only from storybooks or returned missionaries. Jews we had of course heard of—in the Bible!

I hope you get the picture: we were not only "Christians," we were Anglo-Saxon Christians—in jargonese, WASPS. It would have been unusual for anybody in our bailiwick even to announce that he or she was a Lutheran or a Baptist. There were communities of Lutherans, Mennonites, and others fairly nearby; but that's another thing one needs to remember: twenty-five miles was a considerable distance for most of us in those days. We denizens of Oxford County were ready to let the people in the neighboring county, say, in the city of Kitchener (called Berlin before the Great War!) be Lutherans, so long as they weren't subversives—which, during the two world wars, many of us darkly suspected they were. But even the older, highly developed parts of the country were in a practical (not, of course, legal) sense "partitioned" at that time in a way that is hard for people of your generation to envisage.

As for atheism or agnosticism, it lived only in the secret hearts of people. I don't remember anyone ever actually talking as if there might not be a God—other than my father, that is. In my adulthood I have learned how to be grateful for my father's skepticism (he was always asking us, "How do you know?"). But in my childhood and adolescence I was embarrassed by it, and I fought it, because it was definitely "against the stream" in our still-apparently religious atmosphere.

So you are right: I grew up "Christian," and it would have been extraordinary if I had grown up any other way, given the circumstances.

But I doubt very much if the Christianity with which I grew up could ever have carried me through until today. In fact, I know it couldn't have. Already as a young teenager I began to find it flawed, to say the least. Partly, I suppose, my sense of its inadequacy was due to my father's insistent questioning. I fought him at home, but I became his defender and advocate outside the home. Far more

Growing Dissatisfaction

important a factor in my growing dissatisfaction with that Christianity, however, was my own sense of the discrepancy between what the leading people of the church said and the way they actually behaved. That and (this may surprise you) . . . the Bible.

Contradiction

About the discrepancy: I think we should never underestimate the capacity of the human mind, including the mind of the child and adolescent, to sense contradiction. It is probably the greatest hope of the race, humanly speaking. I remember meeting a young man from a communist country in the 1970s. He had become disillusioned with the system and, at great risk, escaped into western Europe, where I was living at the time. I asked him who had helped him see the flaws in doctrinaire Marxism-Leninism—his parents? (No, they were party members); perhaps a teacher at school? (Impossible! They were carefully watched); friends? (Not really). How then had the young man grown so skeptical as to risk his life getting out of that ideological prison? "I began to notice," he said, "the contradiction between what they said about the 'new society' and the way it actually was."

The truth is, the leading lights of my Christian village were, with exceptions, not very admirable people. One of my later teachers of theology, Reinhold Niebuhr, used to say that "the saints ought to be at least as decent as ordinary folk." Too many of our village saints were moralistic, self-righteous, unforgiving human beings. It was not pleasant to be with them. Unfortunately, they were also usually the most successful citizens, economically speaking. They could always impress others with their stern morality because it seemed to pay off. Besides, since they controlled the administration of the township as well as much of the employment of the area, it was practically impossible to cross them. (I am talking, you see, about "Christian establishment" in its concrete American and Canadian expression a few years back. Christianity was never legally established among us, as it was in Europe, but it was very hard, all the same, to draw the line between church and society, religious and secular authorities, genuinely Christian teachings and the guiding principles of the most successful citizens.)

Bible

But with the phrase "genuinely Christian teachings," I have introduced the second and (for me) most important factor in my disillusionment with the Christianity of my environment: the Bible. This obviously requires a little explanation.

You see, in those days (they seem so distant now, but in historical terms half a century isn't very long) Sunday Schools were still taken rather seriously. Nearly everybody I knew attended Sunday School in one of the two village churches, even adults; and in those schools you didn't just color pictures or discuss your "feelings." Even in relatively liberal denominations like ours, "lessons" were based, at least ostensibly, on biblical texts. In the older classes, whole passages of Scripture, and over time whole books of the Bible, were read. Usually, of course, these texts became pretexts for the promulgation of "the usual stuff"—that is, the predictable pietism of teachers representative of the village hierarchy. But since the actual biblical texts were there in our lesson books, the Bible could now and then make itself felt independently of our religious environment.

So when, much later in my life, I learned from my seminary teachers that the Bible is a subversive piece of writing, I knew what they were talking about. It has been the happy fate of Protestantism, which insisted on the "sole authority" of Scripture, to have to live with these writings, like it or not. Nothing has been more subversive of human "religious" tendencies than this book, because the truth is (as a leading theologian of our epoch put it) that "the Bible hates religion." Listen—

> I hate, I despise your feasts,
>   and I take no delight in your solemn assemblies.
> Even though you offer me your burnt offerings
>   and cereal offerings,

I will not accept them. . . .
Take away from me the noise of your songs;
to the melody of your harps I will not listen.
But let justice roll down like waters. . . . (Amos 5:21-24)

The "religion" masquerading as Christianity in my village did not entail the ritual sacrificing of bulls and the like that the prophet Amos condemns in this prophetic blast; it was just plain old village moralism—a simplistic and, in the end, misleading and, often enough, a destructive moralism. (I like Robert Burns's assessment of it: "Morality, thou deadly bane/Thy tens o'thou-sands thou hast slain!") All the weight of tradition, symbol, hymns, prayers, sermons issued finally in this moralism: "Be good and you'll be o.k." And we were not left to work out what "good" might mean all on our own, I can assure you! What it meant, in brief, was conforming to the patterns of respectable behavior set by those same leading Christian citizens. If you stayed within those bounds you could surely succeed—on earth, at least, but probably in heaven too.

I suppose I must have been a little excessive (I know my teenage friends often thought so), but something in me really wanted to be good. Not in the sense of conforming to a social stereotype, but in some deeper way that I myself didn't really understand. Maybe it was because I was the eldest of six children—I'm sure the psychol-ogists could find many reasons for it. "Try to make something of your life," my grandmother wrote in one of her letters to me. But the trouble was, whenever I did the good deeds they told me I should do, I was troubled by a bad conscience more accusatory than ever. For instance, I would make every effort to help some-body—go out of my way to carry an old lady's groceries, or smile at some stranger, or (unlike my little brothers!) work hard around the house. And then this uninvited feeling of guilty smugness would steal over me—like the little boy in the nursery rhyme who "stuck in his thumb and pulled out a plum, and said, 'What a good boy am I!'"

They didn't tell me in Sunday School or church what to do about that. About _pride._ The kind of pride that only the good can entertain—and regularly do.

By my midteens, I had begun to think that Christianity was a pretty shallow business. Its prescriptions for life seemed to me little more than thin, vaguely "sacred" versions of the kind of thing one could hear from all sorts of other sources—schoolteachers, parents, books and stories for the young, agents of the law, even the movies that we occasionally saw, which (in those high days of Grade B Hollywood films) easily distinguished between the good and the bad and always ended with the vindication of the former. Religion didn't appear to have much to say to the likes of me—a boy on the verge of adulthood, hoping that his life might indeed (as Gram had counseled) count for something, but already so introspective, so confused about good and evil, so determined to get behind mere appearances, that he was looked upon by his contemporaries as an odd sort of kid, old before his time, an outsider, a loner.

It was the Bible that made me alter that assessment of Christianity—and of myself!

Gradually I began to realize that the story that the Bible told—its way of picturing the world, human life, God—was quite different from the story that I was being told in and around church. The Bible's heroes were not in fact, as I had been led to think, very heroic, its "good people" were not very good, its saints were not very saintly—not, at least, according to the definitions of goodness and holiness that had conditioned my education in the faith to date.

I remember, for example, an argument I had with one of our ministers over the character of the Old Testament "hero," Jacob (see Genesis 25 and following). The minister insisted that Jacob was a good person, obedient to God, the kind of human being one could respect. After all, he was in the Bible! But, rebel that I was, I couldn't agree. This Jacob, I insisted, was a cheat and a liar: he deceived his old father in order to steal what really belonged to his brother. The minister was a fine person, an authentic gentleman. Had he been as fine a biblical and theological scholar as he was a human being, he might have used the opportunity to introduce his young parishoner to a Book that is beyond village moralism.

There are no absolutely "good" people within the pages of the Bible. Even Jesus—and, not incidentally, in that same passage about the young man who wanted to find "eternal life"—rejects the adjective *good* when it is applied to himself. The young man had addressed him as "Good Teacher," and Jesus immediately retorted, "'Why do you call me good? No one is good but God alone'" (Mark 10:18). Paul sums up the whole human condition with words taken from the prophet Isaiah: "None is righteous, no, not one" (Rom. 3:10). The trouble is, as he puts it in another place, while we may want to be good, in the end our goodness is so mixed up with evil that we can't claim, any of us, to be above reproach. I began to think that the Bible would have agreed more with a certain poem, attributed to Joaquin Miller (1841–1913), I'd heard quoted than with my Sunday School teachers—

> There is so much good in the worst of us,
> And so much bad in the best of us,
> That it hardly behooves any of us
> To talk about the rest of us.

Had my understanding of life remained at this level of thinking, as I now know was the case with many of my contemporaries, I would have ended in a more or less benevolent humanism. And that, I would still say, would have been a great improvement over the petty moralism by which my boyhood life was plagued. But as it happened, the Bible wanted to take me farther.

And I'm very glad it did. Because humanism, benevolent and humane as it may be, leaves too many human questions unanswered. As a way of life it can be superior to dogmatic religion and rigid morality, which too easily resolve life's contradictions and ambiguities; but the more tolerant attitude that humanism cultivates in people doesn't touch the blinding challenges that life throws up at us. Such as, "How can I find eternal life?"—that biblical young man's question, which, being translated into contemporary terms might read: How can I find some sense of meaning, some vocation that will take me out of myself, some relief from my incessant self-examination, some trust in the purposefulness of this whole enterprise called life? So far, the Bible had done for me the necessary preliminary debunking: it had made it clear that real Christianity was *not* this "religious" quest for personal righteousness that regularly ended, as I saw all around me, in mere *self-righteousness*. But if I were going to hold onto Christianity at that stage and beyond, the Bible—or something, somebody—would have to show me in a convincing way what real Christian faith *was*, not only what it *was not*.

I remember to this day the discussion-verging-on-argument during which I began to receive a response to that need (emphasis on *began*; I'm still on the receiving end!). The setting: the young men's class in our Sunday School. Yes, young men, men between sixteen and thirty years of age or so, were still going to Sunday School then in our little corner of Christendom. And we were still expected to read and discuss passages of Scripture. That particular Sunday, the Scripture in question was from Paul—I can't remember whether it was Paul's Romans 1:17, "The just shall live by faith," or Ephesians 2:8-9: "For by grace you have been saved through faith; and this is not your own doing, it is the gift of God—not by works, lest any man should boast."

Now, you are a little older and more knowledgeable than I was at that stage, and you know perfectly well that precisely these verses are at the heart of the Protestant Reformation of the sixteenth century. You've learned in my classes on the history of Christian thought that this idea of "justification by grace through faith," Luther's great "discovery," is the positive teaching that gave many

Christians at the end of the Middle Ages, when Christianity was in crisis, the courage to begin again—to go beyond the worn-out dogmatism and moralism of *that* particular age.

But please believe me, I had no knowledge of any of that! You could easily be a "Protestant" in our part of the world and never have heard of Luther's teaching about grace and faith, or Calvin's understanding of sin—though the Presbyterians in our midst seemed quite aware that they were among the Elect! I suppose that someone in my childhood and youth must have mentioned the names of these reformers, but they were certainly not prominent in our list of saints and heroes. As for their ideas, having since spent three-quarters of my life exposing myself to these ideas I can assure you: they were basically unheard-of in our village. We did hear occasionally about John Wesley, who, as I later found out, was also inspired by these Pauline ideas, but it was his sanctity, not his theology, to which our clergy and others wanted to direct our attention. The truth is, given other (Irish or French) names, and different church interiors and symbols and rituals, and slightly different moral codes, what we supposed Protestants were imbibing as Christianity in our little village was only externally distinguishable from what contemporary Roman Catholics were imbibing in their villages and towns. It had very little to do with the Reformation.

All the same, *the Book* the Reformers read was right there in front of us in the young men's class; and as the discussion went on that day (for the most part it was no discussion, but a teacherly monologue) I began to feel that I had found a friend in that most neglected of saints, Paul. Our teacher, one of the most stalwart of our church's pillars, was as usual impressing upon us young men the importance of our being decent, serious, law-abiding, responsible Christian gentlemen. Well, I don't say that is the worst sort of thing that we could have heard. Of course not! But we—or at least a few of us—needed to hear something more than that. Young men and women even now can benefit sometimes from moral pep-talks, though for the most part they soon learn how to compartmentalize life's "should-be" and life's "is." But what of the young who aren't so clever about keeping moral strictures in a drawer marked "Sunday"? Who really do want to be serious people, responsible citizens? Who are nevertheless hung up on bad consciences that have as much to do with their apparently good as with their obviously questionable thoughts, words, and deeds? Like me.

So I began—much to the consternation of most of my classmates, who had learned that bored endurance was the best way of passing the time—to take issue with the teacher. I pointed out that our scriptural text was not talking about what we should and should not do. In fact, it was critical of our "good works," because when we use them to "justify" ourselves we are just, well, bragging. The text said, didn't it (?), that what was really important was "faith"?

Reluctantly, the teacher had to agree that that was what this text seemed to be saying. But then he did what (as I later learned) is done pretty regularly by the religious: he turned faith itself into a "work." Certainly we should have it! Certainly we should try to cultivate it! Certainly we should believe in the Bible and God and Jesus and so on. "But remember," he said with a triumphant smile, "faith without works is dead." He was quoting the Epistle of James (2:14ff.), a portion of the Bible far more familiar in our milieu than Romans or Ephesians!

I didn't know how, at that point in my life, to counter him. (I know I have spent a lot of time doing so since!) But that didn't matter, because I had begun to find out something new about that "strange, new world within the Bible," as Karl Barth called it. I had begun to discover a road (to be sure it's "the road less traveled") that went beyond good and evil, beyond morality, beyond dogmas and neat divisions of humanity into sheep and goats. And that is the road that I have kept travelling for a very long time now. I'm still a long way from the end of it. But it has never become boring, and I've never quite succumbed to the temptation to think that it leads nowhere.

If I were asked to name that road, I'd say it is called *grace*; and if I were asked who built it, I'd say Jesus, the Jewish teacher, called by

Christians the Christ—with a great deal of help from the historians, law-givers, prophets, and wise ones of ancient Israel. But that puts us a long way ahead of our discussion, and there are still leftovers from your initial question.

What I have been illustrating for you, however, is what some would call the difference between causes and reasons.[1] I could have done that theoretically, but it seemed to me better to illustrate this difference out of my own concrete human experience.

Why Christian? The *cause* of my being so is without a doubt bound up with the particular circumstances of the human history and society into which I was born. But that "cause" not only did not provide a "reason" big enough to keep me Christian, it provided many reasons why I should forget the whole business! I *was* a Christian, of sorts, by birth; I *became* a Christian because I began to intuit very good reasons for being so; I *am* a Christian because those good reasons, while they are by no means either foolproof or above debate, continue to sustain me. And I mean sustain me in *life*, not just in my professional existence or my membership in the Christian community.

The Christendom into which I was born, as I hope you have come to realize as you listened to my story, no longer exists—pockets and vestiges of it notwithstanding. Few people in the Western world today are "caused" to be Christians by the sheer accident of birth. Many may start out that way, but fewer and fewer find inherited Christianity reason enough to stay Christian. As a result, *the whole burden of the Why? of being a Christian today falls on the side of "reasons."*

So I suspect—and I rather hope, in fact—that our dialogue has not ended. In a real way, it has only begun. How would you like to proceed from here?

Why Jesus?

two

The minute you entered my study yesterday I knew at a glance that you had come armed with some pretty weighty thoughts. I'm always a little nervous when confronted by young people with thoughts. Unlike many of their contemporaries who seem content with diversions, and also unlike many older people whose thinking has grown routine and perhaps jaded, young people caught up in original thought—original at least to them—can be a fearsome challenge to professionals. If you don't think so, visit the nearest college or university campus and watch the interaction of students and professors. Watch the professors especially!

"I've got a lot of questions," you announced, without much ceremony. You had, you said, appreciated the fact that I'd taken our conversation seriously enough to give it so much of my time. What I had written in response to your "outburst," as you put it, certainly cleared up one thing: <u>It takes more than social conditioning to make people Christians in any genuine and lasting sense of the term.</u> "And I guess," you added, "that I <u>assumed</u> too easily that all Christians were just unthinking people, living out the lives their culture created for them, mouthing lines written by somebody else."

But that point of major agreement with my "essay," you went on, didn't eliminate all the problems; in fact it raised some new ones.

"For one thing, I didn't find it easy to identify myself with you when you were my age—or a little younger, actually. You seem to have been preoccupied with trying to be 'good,' and being afraid you weren't really good. You were troubled by guilt feelings or something. I guess I understand that," you said, "though I suspect few people ever feel guilty about being too proud of their supposed goodness! But I have to confess that guilt of any kind is not where it's at with me; and I doubt if most of my contemporaries are terribly bothered in that way. We (they call us Generation X, after all!) are more concerned about finding something to do—well, even something to be—than we are about our moral condition."

"My intention in dwelling on my own religious struggle," I responded, "was not to say that it's everybody's struggle, but only to illustrate from my experience the difference between being, on the one hand, born into a so-called Christian culture and, on the other hand, finding reasons for being a Christian that outlast adolescence. I know very well that the specifics of other people's experiences will differ from mine—especially when the historical situation is quite different, as it is with you and your generation. But—well, we can talk about that. Do you want to do that now?" I asked.

"No, let's leave that for another time. There's something that has to come first—or so it seems to me. It's this business about . . . Jesus."

You paused there and looked down. It wasn't embarrassment, I knew; just confusion. Your face said, "Where to begin? So many problems associated with that name!"

"Sometimes," you stammered, "I feel like J. D. Salinger's Holden Caulfield—I can't stand Jesus! You hear the name all over the place. In spite of what you said about Christendom being over, Jesus sure doesn't seem to have disappeared! You turn on the TV or radio and some evangelist or other is intoning that name. I even find the way they say it maddening—'Gee-zus'—as if the very syllables had some magic power in them to reach out and take you by the throat!"

We could both chuckle at that, so you had to admit you knew I was not in that camp. "But all the same," you said, "you put a lot of stock in that name yourself. When you spoke about the reason for your *being a Christian as distinct from the* cause, *you came pretty quickly to Jesus—said he was the builder of the road you travel. . . ."*

You paused again, collecting yourself. Then: "I suppose if people call themselves Christians it's got to have something *to do with Jesus, with . . . 'Christ.' But listen, you and I live in a city where half the people traveling on the buses and subways, among the so-called visible minorities especially, evidently don't link God with Jesus but with the Buddha, or Mohammed, or somebody else. Many of my acquaintances are Hindus, Jews, Sikhs, and so on—apart from the ones that aren't anything at all, religiously speaking, or maybe Christians-twice-removed.*

"So what I want to know is, Why Jesus? In the first place, I'm not convinced even believing in God *is possible today. Why make it even more complicated by asking people to believe in Jesus? By throwing 'the Trinity' at them, for God's sake! And the Virgin birth. And the resurrection from the dead. Does God really need all that? Do we?*

"Besides, isn't it rather strange associating God (I mean, God!) with a person who not only lived so long ago but for all intents and purposes was a loser? Dead at thirty-something? Rejected by nearly everybody, even his own followers? Crying out in pain and loneliness from his cross? Isn't that a contradiction of everything we've been taught to think about God?

"It's certainly contrary to everything our society tells us we should aim for ourselves: success, happiness, 'meaningful' relationships, living full, healthy lives and a peaceful death at a ripe old age—oh, as old as possible! What sort of model for human life is this Jesus, anyway? What decent, middle-class parents would want that for their offspring?"

You were in fine form that morning. A real warrior! And my old armor was vulnerable. I know I didn't do justice to your challenges—though I said a few things that surprised even me. "New" things, in a manner of speaking. Because thought, when it is genuine and passionate, begets thought in others. That's what keeps teachers going: now and then the thought of their students elicits new bursts of originality in old and often tired minds. So once again I pondered what you said for two or three days, and then I wrote the following.

The Scandal (and Necessity!) of Particularity

To begin with, you are right when you say that people are Christians because Jesus is basic to their belief. Of course, since Christianity has for so long played the role of established religion in the West, a good deal of what is called Christian doesn't have anything vital to do with Jesus. You can still occasionally hear people in our society using the adjective *Christian* as if it just meant "Western" (as in "Christian West") or "virtuous person" ("She's a good Christian woman"). There are even many people who have no connection at all with Christianity but are insulted if it is hinted they are not "good Christians." This sort of thing is obviously part of the "vestiges" we talked about already—the "Christendom hangover," so to speak.

Those of us who are serious about this faith, however, know that we can no longer trust such merely conventional, rhetorical associations with Christianity. As I said last time, we are thrown back on "reasons." And at the very center of the *reason* for being Christian there stands this name, a name designating a particular, historical human being—yes, his followers insisted from the beginning, a fully *human* being, just as we are, but one who puts us in touch with God in a way that is unique in our experience.

You may want to ask (some people do), Do we have to be "put in touch with God"? If there is a God, isn't God just somehow "there"? Don't human beings have a natural tendency to think "God," or however they may refer to the Supreme Being, the Something-Behind-It-All, or whatever? Aren't we continuously told that no tribe of Homo sapiens or its forerunners has ever been located that did not worship some deity, often involving very complex mythologies and rituals? So isn't the human being just "religious" by nature? Couldn't you even name our species *Homo religiosus* [the religious species] just as accurately as *Homo sapiens*? Or maybe more accurately, since our collective "wisdom" (*sapientia*) is more debatable, certainly, than our persistent religiousness?

I'm trying to respond, you see, to what you said about how hard it is even to believe in *God* today. You're right too in making that "today" important. Whatever may have been the case in the past, many observers of our own historical period would want to question the time-honored assumption that human beings are religious "by nature"—as though we were programmed, so to speak, to believe in God. Ever since the Enlightenment of the eighteenth century, it has been possible, apparently, for increasing numbers of men and women to live without any religion. I am not referring only to a few radical atheists who boast that they do not need the "God hypothesis," or who say with Nietzsche that "God is dead." I mean that a great many ordinary people in the nineteenth and twentieth centuries have *lived* as if God were absent from their lives. "There ain't no George," one such person said to me (it was his rejoinder to the old saying, "Let George do it."[1] In case you miss the allusion, he meant: "There ain't no *God*, you have to *do it* all by yourself—with maybe (as the song suggests) 'a little help from your friends.'"

We're talking, in other words, about a kind of working atheism, or at least ordinary secularism. It has been very widespread. It was present already in my village during my youth, despite the appearance of religion. Lately, to be sure (I mean within the past decade or two), this without-God-ism (the literal meaning of *a-theism*) has become somewhat nervous about itself. It isn't nearly so self-confident as it was in the earlier part of this century. We are less certain of our own *human* ability to "do it," so some of us are more open to God-talk than was the case thirty or forty years ago.

But that means that we are also having once again to confront the *big* question—which is not really (as the old atheism supposed) whether God *exists*, but what God, if God exists, is *like*! Not *whether* God is, but *who* God is.

I don't mean that the question of God's existence is unimportant, of course. But, in the first place, I doubt if anyone ever comes to believe in God (as distinct from believing that God exists) as a result of some theoretical argument, like those of Thomas Aquinas; and, in the second place, it makes all the difference in the world what *sort* of deity a person believes in. Some of the gods people believe in are harmless enough; others present enormous social as well as personal problems. Think about Jonestown, or Waco, or the "Heaven's Gate" cult. Think about the gods that sanction racism and sexism and war. Think too about the gods that make people so fixated on "heaven" that they don't care at all about the fate of the earth, only about their own personal "salvation"—which unfortunately is what much of the Christianity on this continent amounts to still today.

In short, the really important question that has to be put to all believers in deity is, *What exactly do you mean by God?* Human history is full of divinities of every conceivable sort. New gods are being trotted out every minute of the day. North America is one of the most fertile breeding grounds in the world for new divinities—often enough (to the embarrassment of informed Christians) they are labeled Christian! An extraterrestrial visitor to planet Earth would surely find it mind-boggling to observe what the so-called "wise species" will bow down, and how easy it is for "true believers" of *whatever* persuasion to gather a following. The Bible, which as I said last time is remarkably suspicious of "religion," teaches us to be particularly cautious in the presence of the claim to belief in "God," because it is realistic about the fantastic variety of meanings that that universally used term has, many of them terribly questionable from its vantage point. It knows all about the child-abusing gods and the sex-crazed gods and the gods zealous for their own omnipotence and the sweet-talking gods who condone whatever you want to do. In a real way, it says of the gods what Jesus once said about human beings and systems: You will recognize them for what they really are by their "fruits." That is, test the gods by the behavior of their followers.

In at least this respect, biblical faith shares something in common with all of the great world religions (by which, I suppose, we could mean religions that have stood the test of time): They all recognize the need for definition and for limits in relation to deity. They therefore associate the common term or concept "God" with some particular manifestation, revelation, or exemplification of God that is closer to human experience and more definitive than is the abstract notion of a supreme being. To say the same thing in other words, all of these religions have their *particulars* through which they explain the *universal* that in the English language we term *God*.

Forgive me for using this sort of terminology, but you need not be daunted by it. It may not be the *language* you use every day, but it describes the *life* you live every day, all the same. For instance, if you are like most of us you probably think that Love is important for Happiness, and that the education of Children matters for the Future of the Race, and that Women should have equal opportunity with Men, and so on. Well, all the words that I capitalized in that sentence are universals—that is, they name something larger than the specific examples of it known to us. Without universal concepts or ideas of this sort, human communication and even human thought as such would not be possible. We would all live in our own separate language shells, if we had such a thing as language in the first place—which we probably wouldn't.

And yet all universal concepts (love, childhood, woman, man, sorrow, and so on) acquire whatever concrete meaning they have for us only as we experience particular embodiments or instances of them. To illustrate: I have never experienced Love in some theoretical, disembodied way; I learned about love by being loved and by loving particular human and extrahuman (dogs, cats, trees) beings. Or again, you will not meet Childhood on any street of any city, but you will meet children; and the particular children you come to know and love during your life will provide the universal idea of "Childhood" with some specific significance for you. The children of your experience will not exhaust the whole meaning of "Childhood," because you will realize that there are countless millions of other children, past, present, and future, whom you do not and could not know. All the same (and I have learned this mainly through the poignant, and often fearful, but in the end glorious, experience of being the father of four such!), the particular children who are part of your life will prevent the universal concept of "the Child" from being just a concept, a term, an abstraction.

And this, hopefully, will have an *ethical* effect on you, because, the particular children in your life having made the whole idea of childhood something concrete and vital to you, you will not be able to remain indifferent when (for instance) you hear about the evils of child prostitution or the scandalous rate of child poverty in our "developed" society, and so on. Because you will have loved those *particular* children, your consciousness of childhood *universally* will have been awakened in ways that could not have occurred if you had lived in isolation from children.

Now, the concepts *Deity*, or *Divinity*, or *God* are also universals in the sense that they are used everywhere in one form or another to designate what people believe is ultimate; and the universally used idea "God" (or its equivalents) is just as abstract and ill-defined as any other universal concept unless and until it is associated with some particular being, event, writing, art, experience, or what-have-you. That is why Buddhism associates the ultimate with the Buddha, and Islam with Mohammed and the Koran, and Hinduism with a whole pantheon of very specific beings, and Bahai with Baha-Ullah, and Judaism with Abraham and the Torah and the prophets. . . .

And it is the reason why God in *Christian* belief is inseparable from . . . Jesus. Despite their terrible complications, the basic thought behind all those seemingly hard-to-swallow doctrines that you mentioned in our talk the other day—the Trinity, the

Incarnation, the Virgin Birth, the Resurrection, and so forth—(to put it in the simplest language I know) is that God is like Jesus. Or (in conventional Christian terms) that God is "revealed" by Jesus. Or (as I said here earlier) that Jesus "puts us in touch with God" in a unique and decisive way. Christianity came into existence only when and because some people, at first all of them Jews, believed that—that is, when they felt that they had experienced the presence of God in a new and compelling way through their contact with Jesus. And, as we already both agreed, there is no other legitimate reason for calling oneself a Christian. After all, the term *Christian* refers to someone who confesses that Jesus is "the Christ," the "Messiah," that is, the one awaited and yearned for; the one through whom the deepest longings of life are met and responded to.[2]

Now, to make Jesus so very basic to what one means by "God" is of course to engage in choice, a choice that will seem arbitrary to many others; and it is to take a risk—the risk that the One responsible for all that is, the Creator and Sovereign of the universe, is like (or at least not essentially different from) this historically conditioned, and therefore limited, finite, mortal human being, Jesus of Nazareth. This is what caused some theologians of our own period to coin the phrase "the *scandal* of particularity." The word *scandal* comes from the newer Testament itself—from Paul, who wrote that the "good news" (gospel) announced by Christians, centered as it is in "Jesus Christ and him crucified," is a *skandalon* to the religious and the wise ones of the world (1 Cor. 1:18f.).

And it *is* a scandal, a stumbling block, especially when (as you so vehemently pointed out) it means that Christians link God with "a loser," a failed teacher, a human being executed by the state for subversive activity. Later we can talk about what that means, but for now we will just observe the fact that it is—to say the least!—an exceptionally provocative idea. And Christians shouldn't forget that and behave and speak as if it were a perfectly reasonable idea—that the "Almighty God" should keep that kind of company, so to speak.

All the same, there is a certain reasonableness about the general *procedure*, if I may put it that way, that Christians are following here; and we should not forget that, either. To associate God with Jesus is in principle just as reasonable as associating Love with your particular lover or associating Childhood with specific children. In all of these instances, all that is happening is that universals are being experienced and explained by particulars. And that is not only a *reasonable* thing, it is a *necessary* thing; for without the particulars the universals remain both unknown, in any profound sense, and so vague as to be lacking in any kind of substance and significance.

Just let me pause a moment and try to give that last sentence a little more weight. I know a young woman, a very fine young woman, full of enthusiasm for life, and imagination, and daring. She was always fond of old people, and of children too. She was never without a special sort of feeling for little kids—partly, I believe, because she was never very far away from her own rather happy childhood. But then one day she gave birth to a baby of her own. And as I observed her over the space of a year or so, I noticed that she had suddenly risen to a whole new level of human awareness and involvement. It was sometimes painful, this new consciousness of hers: she would sit and cry in movies when she saw children treated inconsiderately, and she would spend some nights anxiously thinking and dreaming about what sort of world it was becoming. At the same time, for all the pain of it, she was no longer living a couple of feet above the earth, with her youthful idealism and enthusiasm. Whenever she was tempted to think too high or too low about life, she would tell herself: "I have a baby." Through this little child, she acquired worldly roots and a sense of responsibility for the future of *all* little boys and girls—yes, and dogs and plants and all the rest! She acquired what we may call *compassion*, which seasoned and changed and deepened her natural *passion* for life.

Observing her, I was reminded of what Luther once said about the whole meaning of the Christian message: "The gospel is nothing other than the story of God's little son and of his humbling." If one is caught up in that story, as the young woman became caught up in the life of her child, one experiences a new level of commitment to life that the universal term *God* cannot evoke. So while it is, yes, a scandalous thing to put one's faith in Jesus as God's definitive "particularization," so to speak, it is also consistent with the general necessity within which finite beings like ourselves always live and move, think and feel.

That being said, we come again to the big question: What God? What is this God like? If Jesus "reveals" God, puts us in touch with God, makes God specific and particular, no longer a vague abstraction, then what sort of God do we have here? Is this a God chiefly of power and might, who is primarily concerned for "himself" and "his" own glory? Or is this a God who is out to condemn every sinner—who, as Dorothy Sayers once wrote with characteristic irony, really hated everybody, but let his wrath fall on his beloved son instead? Or is this a legalistic, tit-for-tat sort of God, who has once and for all laid down the rules for being a "good" human being—a moralistic divinity who backs up the moral codes of exemplary citizens (my village!)? Or is this an internalized, gently forgiving, no-hard-feelings sort of God whose "business," as an ironic thinker of the nineteenth century said, "is to forgive"?[3] *If Jesus is for Christians the finite one through whom the Infinite is primarily glimpsed, what does that tell us, concretely, about the Infinite—about "God"?*

Well, at this point, of course, you and I would be best advised to go straight to the Gospels—especially to the so-called "Synoptic

Gospels," Matthew, Mark, and Luke—and see precisely what is recorded there about Jesus: how he behaved toward others—poor people, sick people, women, men of power, children; what he taught his followers about God, life, goodness, evil, other creatures, nature, death, despair, the demonic, hope, and so on; how he handled his own finitude, his obvious limitations, his apparently inevitable and not-distant death; what made him angry, what made him glad . . . in short, as much as we could find out about him. Maybe that wouldn't be as much as we *wanted* to find out— it probably wouldn't be. When so much depends on the Bible's description of him—not only *his* nature and destiny after all, but the whole way one might think about God!—it seems to many people a shame that the newer Testament doesn't tell us more. It tells us less and less, according to some scholars, who find so much of what the Bible does say about Jesus more legend and interpretation than trustworthy historical information. All the same, I'd say, we can learn *enough* about Jesus from the Bible to know *enough* about the God he reveals to enable us to trust what comes to us from less "objective" sources—from tradition, from the church, and also from "the Holy Spirit," about whom we have yet to talk.

At the very least, from the Bible (not just the four Gospels but the epistles and the older Testament too) we can discover enough about the identity, character, intentions, and destiny of Jesus to understand who God, according to this faith tradition, is *not*. And, by the way, isn't our knowledge of persons usually more heavily informed by negation (who and what they aren't) than by position (who and what they are)? I mean, if you ask me to describe my son I could tell you a great many things about him; but if I talked about him for hours I would never nearly exhaust the mystery of who he *is*; because, knowing him, I am conscious of that mystery above all. Wherever the object of our knowledge is no object but a living subject, a person, a "thou," we know that we cannot and must not reduce this person to a thing, an "it"—not even to a thing as seemingly desirable as a relatively accurate description of him or her. Think about that in relation to someone whom you know very well. We can be much more decisive when we describe who somebody close to us is *not* than when we try to define them in strictly accurate, positive terms.

So who is God *not*, then, if Jesus particularizes for us who God is?

That, for certain, is a tall order! I'm going to take a stab at it, partly because the line of my argument up until now demands that, but also because I think it's possible (God permits it, so to speak) to do that sort of thing—provided we don't turn it into an ironclad theory, something written in stone, or what the Bible itself calls a "graven image." In the end Jesus, like everybody else (!), must be given the freedom to define *himself*—who he is, who he isn't—quite independently of our ideas of him. In the end, the only way to *know* Jesus is to encounter him—just as is the case with everybody else. And that, Christians believe, really is possible, strange as it may seem to the strictly literal mind, because for them Jesus is not just confined to a moment in history two thousand years ago, and to the testimony of a few people who met him then, but he belongs to the present and future, too. His Spirit still lives, and still seeks us out—pursues us.

There! I've mentioned the Holy Spirit, and we'll have to consider that important aspect of Christian belief more fully later; but, for now let me just observe that without some "spiritual" experience of Jesus Christ as one present and among us, our knowledge of Jesus would be only historical knowledge, not knowledge of him as *person.* And historical knowledge would not be enough to create faith (trust) in us, nor would it be sufficient to bring into being a whole community of such trust—the church.

For the time being, however, in responding to the question at hand I want to stick to the importance of the biblical witness to Jesus, the particular historical person. As we have already observed about "spiritual" matters and about "religion" as a whole, the danger (human beings being what they are), is that people will make of a merely "spiritualized" Jesus whatever they need or want to make of him, and so we'll end up with the same problem all over again: Who really *is* this Jesus who shows us God? What kind of

God is this? So we can't afford to avoid asking the historical witness to Jesus, the Bible, to help us discern at least who Jesus is _not._
You only have to look around you in North America today to realize how important that is, because nothing is more confusing and
often (as you yourself passionately insisted) more offensive than a
"Jesus" who is little more than the pathetic attempt of little minds
to render their own pet theories and pursuits absolute!

So, more by way of suggestion than anything like completion, let
me say a little about who I think Jesus is *not*—ergo who the God
Jesus puts us in touch with is not:

First, this is *not* a God who is interested mainly in displaying
"his" own power and glory—not a macho deity, so to speak; not
even in the usual sense a "he" (Christian feminists are quite right
about that). It is true that the prayer Jesus taught his disciples to
say ends, in some versions, with the words, "For thine is the kingdom, the power, and the glory"; but, if we consider that statement
alone, not to mention many other texts that could be considered,
we had better note well that the natural emphasis has to fall on the
word *thine*: "*thine* is the glory. . . ." In other words, God defines
what power and glory are, not Caesar, nor Napoleon, nor any of
the seekers after prominence that history has raised up. If power
and glory in the commonly understood sense were the essence of
God, biblically conceived, then God would have to be "particularized" by a very different sort human mediator than Jesus was. A
mediator who is identified with the powerless and inglorious of
the earth; a mediator despised and rejected above all by the powerful and glorious; a mediator whose "kingdom" is made up of
harlots and fishermen and hated tax collectors and broken people—such a mediator is hardly your average monarchic type! Jesus
as the Christ, the representative of God, the "anointed one" is after
something   very   different   from   divine   "all-powerfulness"

(omnipotence), as this is usually conceived of by both politics and religion. And to achieve that something, Jesus is ready to submit to everything that the blood-and-thunder types of every age and clime regularly avoid like the plague: association with "the wrong people," suspicion and ostracization by "the right people," personal poverty, homelessness, propertylessness, humiliation, physical pain, utter social rejection.

In fact, if one thought long enough and hard enough about why Jesus is *not* ambitious for power and glory (though the Bible assures us he could have had it if he had wanted it), one might stumble onto what *God's* power and glory (religion and politics to the contrary!) really *are*. And the surprise of that discovery might be intriguing enough to last a lifetime. Certainly it would carry one into places one had probably not intended to go, along roads one had probably not intended to take (see John 21:18).

Second, the God Jesus reveals is not, cannot be, a God whose main object is to fashion morally upright people—people personally irreproachable, spiritually superior types, so to speak. It could be argued that the Stoics aimed for that sort of thing, but such an explanation doesn't fit the biblical record concerning Jesus.

I know I could be accused of still fighting my youthful battles against the moralists of my village, but for the life of me I can't see how so many alleged Christians in two thousand years of alleged discipleship of Jesus Christ have ended up such moralistic people! Clearly, Jesus' greatest quarrel—greater even than his quarrel with the religious and political powers of his context—was with those contemporaries of his who felt they were honoring God by making themselves out to be morally superior types, like the man in the temple who thanked God he was "not like this tax collector," this "sinner" (Luke 18:9f.). Jesus in the Gospels not only criticizes such pretensions to moral goodness, but he goes out of his way to associate with the reputedly bad people—prostitutes and barkeepers, socially shunned tax collectors, foreigners, adulterers, lepers and other physically and mentally challenged persons, and so on. How can anybody miss the message contained in all that, especially when the biblical Jesus (or his interpreters) actually *says* what the message is so often and so plainly: namely, that God is not interested in outward acts of personal moral uprightness but in the *motives* for our allegedly good behavior and—in one word—our capacity to *love others*: which means what it says, to *love* them, not merely condescend to them; and to love *them*, rather than just loving ourselves for seeming to love them!

And again I'd like to observe that if you pondered this biblical struggle against moralism long enough and hard enough; if you tried to discover *why* that approach to life is rejected, then you might be led to contemplate the highly *positive* thing that is being suggested by this negation. I mean, you might be inspired to wonder about this same love, a love that does not wait for us to become lovable but accepts us and seeks to transform us from the inside out.

That brings me to the *third* point: the criticism of religious moralism I've just expressed should not be turned into an excuse for saying that "anything goes." The God revealed by Jesus of Nazareth is *not*, evidently, just a God who "forgives," that being "his business." Demands are made, commandments are given, and there are consequences for those who ignore these. It is not as if, being liberated from moralistic, legalistic religion, the disciples of Jesus were given *carte blanche*: "You are saved by a love you didn't deserve, so now go and do whatever you please." To the contrary! God's love won't let you go. What sort of love would it be if it did? As with all love, really, God's love comes with strings attached. It binds us to itself. It contains an inherent discipline.

Discipleship is the discipline to which Jesus introduces those whom his love beckons. Following him is not less rigorous than the moralities from which he delivers us; it is more rigorous, because its essence is loving as one has been loved. Really to love others is far more demanding than just "doing good deeds" or "being nice." For most of us, to be honest, it means that we have to stop loving ourselves so much, putting ourselves first; and that is a transformation neither easily nor quickly achieved. It will require a lifetime even to approximate it, and it won't be learned without suffering.

But here I could become too complicated. It's a big topic, and we will no doubt encounter it again. My point just now is only this: against the sort of "anything goes" religion that some have made of Christianity, it has to be said that everything *doesn't* go if you fall into the hands of *this* God, the one particularized by the life and death of Jesus. The generosity and forgiveness and compassion of God should not be interpreted to mean that nothing special is asked of those who are drawn into believing in this God through Jesus' representation of God.

Fourth, the God whom Jesus makes known to us cannot be considered a deity who insists that everybody who wants to be "saved" has got to accept the Christian faith, be baptized, and say the words *Lord* and *Savior*—and, of course, *Jesus*—as often as possible!

Alright, this is important. It's important to you, obviously enough—I'm referring to your outburst the other day, your quite right defense of your friends who are Jewish and Muslim and agnostic and so on. But it's important for all of us today. So I'll have to spend a little more time on it than on the first three points in this "process of elimination."

As Christians become more aware of the plurality of religions, they manifest a tendency to fall into one of two different camps. Labels are usually misleading because they obscure shadings and nuances of belief, but for purposes of discussion we may speak of one camp as "conservative" and the other as "liberal." In relation to the matter of religious plurality, conservative Christianity, fearing that the centrality of Jesus Christ will be compromised, emphasizes all the more adamantly the indispensability of an explicit confession of belief in Jesus as Lord and Savior. Liberal Christianity rejects this as unwarranted exclusivism, maintaining that it is

fundamentally un-Christian because of its intolerance of difference. The liberal preference is to deemphasize or downplay the
role of Jesus in order to be true to the spirit of tolerance and inclusivity that, as liberal Christians feel, Jesus himself exemplified. The
more unavoidable the sociological fact of religious plurality
becomes (and in North American city culture it is increasingly
conspicuous), the more polarized the internal Christian debate
becomes. All Christians today are under a great deal of pressure to
declare themselves, to choose one or the other of these alternatives. Will they risk being thought prejudiced and bigoted by opt-
ing for the exclusive saviorhood of Jesus? Or will they risk being
accused of relativism or indecision, or worse, by assigning Jesus a
less exclusive role in salvation?

But is that really the choice before us? Are there only these two
possibilities—either you extol Jesus by excluding everybody who
doesn't actually name that name, or you minimize his place in
Christian faith in order to appear more accepting and inclusive?

There is another way of thinking about all this that avoids both
doctrinaire exclusivism and doctrinaire inclusivism, and in the
process is also far more faithful to biblical claims. Let's go back to
what we observed about the relation between universals and particulars. We certainly didn't diminish the significance (in fact, we
called it the "necessity")—of the particular person, Jesus of
Nazareth, called "the Christ" by his followers. At least we didn't
pursue the ultraliberal route of presenting Jesus as one among
many revealers of the transcendent and mysterious God, *possibly*
the most important. But neither did we pursue the ultraconservative route of limiting everything about the transcendent and mysterious God to what we think about Jesus. Jesus, being a real person, we insisted, is in the first place not reducible to our thoughts
and doctrines about him—our "Christologies." Moreover, if it is
really God whom Jesus reveals, then we must assume that God,
too, is Person—is the Eternal Thou, as Martin Buber insisted, One
who resists the tendency of human beings to reduce deity to an It,
to something readily definable. Something we can possess! Over

against all preconceptions and all clear-cut dogmas and definitions, the biblical God announces, "I will be who I will be"[4] *Yahweh*
In fact, what is so fascinating about the "necessary," if "scandalous," *particular* named Jesus is that, being person, he puts us in
touch with a *universal*, God, who as living Person transcends our
ideas and images of the divine *in the very act of coming close to us.*
The newer Testament announces that Jesus is "Emmanuel, which
means, God-with-us" (Matt. 1:23). Yet it presents Jesus as one who
never flaunts his own relation to God, never boasts of his "divinity," never pretends to be or to contain God fully. On the contrary,
as one of the great epistles of the newer Testament concludes, Jesus
"emptied himself" (Phil. 2:5ff.) of all such extravagant claims—
claims that are characteristically made by figures believing themselves to be specially chosen vehicles of the divine! Indeed, Jesus
never even openly claims the title "Christ" for himself. When the
apostle Peter, with typical impetuosity, confesses that he believes
Jesus to be, in fact, the promised Messiah, Jesus charges his disciples not to talk about this (Mark 8:29f.; Luke 9:20f.), even though
he tells Peter that his impulsive confession has been inspired by
God (Matt. 16:13-20). Contrary to later (and usually heretical)
Christologies, Jesus as he is depicted in the Gospels and epistles of
the newer Testament, does not wish to be considered (as it were)
all the God of God there is. That is why he addresses God as his
"Abba" (a familiar designation for "Father"; Mark 14:36)—the
"one God" of Israel to whom, as an faithful Jew, he prays, and
whose will he struggles to understand and obey, even if obedience
has to mean losing his own life—which in the end it does.

As you consider this biblical testimony to Jesus, please remember what we said about particulars as a whole: they never fully *contain* the universals that they represent or embody, even though we
could never *know* the universals without them. The specific children we come to know and love, we said, make the concept "childhood" explicit and concrete enough for us that we are able to open
ourselves more fully to *all* children—even, in many cases, to the
point of neglecting our own children for the sake of children

whose need is greater than that of our own. To say it more techni-
cally, the function of particulars is to draw our attention *to* themselves in order that they may at the same time point *beyond* themselves. This doesn't mean that particulars are unimportant in and
for themselves. That young woman of my illustration earlier certainly did not treat her baby as a mere *channel* to something
greater; but all the same that is precisely what her baby did for her:
that one little child came close enough to her life to turn her in a
new and profound way toward the whole world of children—
indeed, toward the whole world as such!

Jesus, if he is for us what he can and should be, does not cut us
off from others but, precisely by being there at the center of our
confession of faith in God, opens our minds and hearts *to* others—including (certainly!) those others who do not name *him*,
Jesus, as their redeemer, their doorway to the eternal. I can say
without any doubt at all that I am far more open to Jews and Muslims and Sikhs and humanists and all kinds of other human
beings, including self-declared atheists, *because* of Jesus than I
should ever have been *apart* from him. Precisely part of what I, for
one, would have to mean by "salvation" is being saved from the
seemingly "natural" but ultimately very destructive tendency of
human beings to distrust and exclude others, especially those who
are *obviously* "other." But here I am already verging on a subject
that we shall have to look into more closely: "salvation." So let me
just conclude this with the following observation:

If you say enough about who someone is *not*, you create by a
process of elimination a kind of space within which to contemplate the question, "Who then *is* this person, really?" This applies
to every person: as I said, in the end persons must be left at liberty
to identify *themselves*. The purpose of our eliminating these four
characteristics from our picture of Jesus, and so of the God Jesus
reveals, is not just to end there—with a negative definition. It is
only to prepare the way, as it were, for Jesus himself to identify
himself—to encounter us *in all the clarity and mystery of his being.*

Saved from What?— For What?

three

"It seems," you began, "that every time some question I have about the 'why?' of Christian faith is answered, new questions crop up. Your piece on Jesus helped me to understand a little better how Christians can justify putting so much of an emphasis on him. But I still don't see what they mean by thinking of him as their 'Savior.' I guess I don't even know what they mean by 'being saved.'"

"But you probably hear that phrase being used quite often," I suggested. "Perhaps you have some friends who use it? [You nodded.] Don't they help you to understand what it means?"

"Oh, some of them throw the term 'born again' around, and a few other standard phrases," you replied, "though they don't say much about what these phrases actually mean. I get the impression it's a kind of code language—the way they recognize one another, or something! . . . And then, well, you can hardly avoid hearing about 'being saved' with (what is it?) thirty percent of Americans claiming that status for themselves! But, frankly, I find all this pretty strange. Some of these people are just my age and they're already turned on by the idea of getting to heaven. I'm not in the least interested in getting to heaven. In fact, I'm doing everything I can to avoid it! So when I hear these 'saved' people talking and singing and shouting about how great it will be when they are dead and in heaven I have to wonder:

What must they think about this life if they're so enthusiastic about wrapping it up and getting on with the next one? If that's what salvation is, then I say forget it!"

"Maybe you'll be more interested in heaven forty or fifty years from now," I suggested, drawing just a little on my own temptations.

"Maybe," you agreed. "But I hope I'm not. I hope that when I'm seventy or eighty—if I'm lucky enough to get that far—I'll still feel rooted in this life. Too many older people in my experience tend to give up on the world. Just at the point where they could be of some use to those of us who are just beginning our journey, they take off for heaven—or Florida!"

That's exactly what I like so much about you. I'm not romantic about Youth, capital Y. Not all young people demonstrate your kind of passion for life. There are bored and cynical young people, too. But somehow one feels that this world, if it's ever going to be loved, will have to be loved first by the young; and when one hears one of their number affirming life so unconditionally as you were doing then, one is spontaneously glad. It helps some of us who are no longer young to fight our own temptations—temptations to disillusionment and apathy and plain grumpiness! Well, and to being seduced by "heaven," too. Is it perhaps not quite accidental that the one Christians call "Savior" was a young person?

"I wouldn't even bother with this subject," you went on, "if it depended on what I hear from the noisy 'born-agains.' But I sensed in some of the things you've said that there might be a different angle on it. For instance, in what you gave me to read after our last talk you hinted that salvation would have to mean something like saving us from our fear and mistrust of other people."

I acknowledged I had said something like that—"But I don't intend to limit the meaning of 'salvation' or 'redemption' or whatever else it might called to one of its consequences."

"I gathered that, of course," you said. "So today I'd like us to talk about what salvation means at its most basic. What is the central thing—the thing from which such 'consequences,' as you call them, might follow? I mean, what are we saved from, would you say, and *for what purpose—what* for? *And then, how is all that connected with Jesus?"*

That was certainly clear enough. I couldn't think of a better way of stating the question. But you still hadn't finished laying out the problem. You reminded me of the first discussion we had had, and how, afterwards, I had written about the way that Christianity had come to make sense to me. "The reason you gave for that," you said, "had something to do with your sense of being forgiven—accepted. Was I right when I said, last time, that you had strong feelings of guilt?"

"Not in the way that that is usually understood," I answered. "I certainly wasn't overwhelmed by guilt. I don't remember moping about with anything as overpowering as a 'guilt-complex.' Thanks to my parents and many other people, my adolescence and youth were basically happy, even 'normal,' whatever that may mean. If I gave you the impression that I felt deeply judged by the moral expectations of our village church leaders, that was a false impression. I was always too skeptical about the legitimacy of their moralism to give it that kind of prominence in my life.

"If at another, inward level I felt 'guilty'—or let's say not quite right, not 'genuine' or something—it had more to do with my own expectations than anybody else's. My unease was more immediately related to my no doubt idealistic attempts at being 'good' than with any moral misdemeanors of which I was conscious. I felt that it should be possible, somehow, to be good—think good thoughts, perform good acts—without feeling so damn good about being good! So smug. In other words, I worried more about what I thought of as my unwarranted egoism than about any little obvious wrongs that I could be accused of (of which, I suppose, there were enough).

"And what made all that so complicated for me at the time was that nobody else seemed to know what I was talking about. Even my close friends, when I tried to explain about my stupid pride, would tell me that I was being too hard on myself. Some said that having a good feeling about one's good deeds was God's way of rewarding us. I never bought that argument, and I'm glad I didn't. Pride really is the most subtle form of sin. It latches onto all the seemingly positive things we can conjure up about ourselves and gives us a bloated self-image. When as a young man I felt remorse for that pride, I was closer to the Bible's view of what's wrong with us human beings than I knew at the time.

"So, to answer your question in the way that you have asked it, I'd have to say that it was exactly that self-conscious pride—that absorption with self—that I had to be saved from. And as to what I was saved for, I think the best word would be 'freedom': freedom from self-preoccupation, freedom for others, freedom to enter into life more joyously, less cautiously."

"And did you do that?" you asked.

"I've never become free enough, of course—in that sense," I told you. "I'm afraid I keep sliding back into self-concern—worrying about myself, congratulating myself, examining myself, blaming myself, and so on. But I am pretty sure, all the same, that if I had never heard the Christian message, never experienced anything that could be called 'salvation,' I'd likely be even more self-centered today than I am. I could well have become a lifelong neurotic, so bound up with myself that I wouldn't have begun to find out what life is all about. I really think that 'salvation,' when it's for real, must have something to do with freeing us from the burden of self-absorption, freeing us for—well, for love, in a word. That seems to me pretty basic."

We were silent for awhile after that—I remembering, you considering. But you still had your agenda, obviously enough; and I didn't want to sidetrack it by insisting that we should right away pursue the line I had introduced. I realized I had gotten carried away. I'd thrown in my own "answer" to your question too soon—before I had given you the chance to elaborate on your question.

"I can see," you observed after awhile, "that what I was going to say about guilt doesn't fit your story very well, or at least not in a direct way. But it does, I think, describe the situation of quite a few people who talk about sin and salvation; so I'd like to have your reaction to it.

"What I mean is this: When they speak about salvation and don't just mean 'getting to heaven,' many Christians seem to be saying that *what they've been saved from is the terrible consequences of their sinful, guilty past—terrible, maybe, even to the extent of sending them to hell instead of heaven.*

"I'll admit that what you've just said about your own experience of sin and salvation is different—maybe a lot different. I guess what I want now is to find out just how it's different. And maybe one way of doing that would be to have you comment on what I've noticed about the people who use this sin-and-salvation language. Why, would you say, is it so tied up with either getting to heaven, or being saved from hell because of one's guilt?

"Let me tell you again why I ask this: I already said that I've very little interest in getting to heaven, at least not now. But I'm also not worried about hell, frankly. I mean (and I think I already said this to you before), I don't feel all that guilty. I'd be very surprised—I think I'd even be indignant—if anybody told me that the things I've done in my twenty-odd years, or even the things I haven't done, are serious enough to deserve eternal damnation or something.

"I'll have to think about what you said—about pride and all that. But at the moment I can't even think that I've been overly proud, or egoistic. At least I know I haven't been worried about that, or felt any serious qualms about it. And, given my background as a modern, middle-class city kid, I don't know how I could have ended up at twenty-something with a guilt-complex of any kind, unless my story were pretty unusual. I mean, you, back there in your little village, were up against a society—a rather single-minded society, according to your own testimony—that had very clear-cut rules and regulations. You would have known from Day One what was expected of you. But with me and most of my contemporaries, on the contrary, all that is much more vague. Really fuzzy! Our city culture today is full of all sorts of different lifestyles. It's almost a case of 'take your pick.' I mean, my world is a lot more tolerant than yours was, a lot more open. . . ."

"Do you think," I interjected, "that it's perhaps too open?"

"That could be," you admitted, pausing again to consider the possibility. "Yes, it could be. I mean, I like the fact that our society is

open—you know, that there are different possibilities. I wouldn't want to live in a world where everything is laid out in advance. But there is, it's true, a downside to our openness, too. Because if you're given the impression you can do, basically, whatever you want, then after awhile you may begin to wonder whether anything at all is expected of you. Is it all just an aimless game, whose only goal is to win—win at sex, or in the ongoing competition for the best one-liners, or getting A's, or being cool? Believe me, in spite of what many people in your generation think of mine, there are some of us who find those kinds of goals as trivial as some of you do."

Another pause—a long one this time. Then: *"Your society back then may have been problematic—you yourself said it was. But at least you knew what was expected of you, and I gather it wasn't just the usual middle-class success story you were fed. In relation to that story, one can feel a failure, but not guilt. In one of my classes last year we had to read Kafka's* The Trial. *Most of us hadn't the vaguest idea what Kafka was getting at—the mysterious guilt of his anti-hero, Herr K.*

"So there you are," you concluded. *"I don't hanker for heaven, and I'm not afraid of hell. I don't worry much about death, and I don't feel guilty. How can 'salvation' mean anthing to me?"*

"What do *you* feel? What are *you* worried about?" I asked, hoping you would expand a little what you were saying about the lack of "expectations." "I don't mean daily worries, this and that. I mean in general, overall. When you think about your life, your future, and so on, is there anything like a recurring anxiety?"

"What I do feel sometimes—well, fairly often, actually—is . . . how to put it? Superfluous, I guess. Who needs me? A large number of my contemporaries can't even find any decent work—not any work at all, some of them. And they tell us that that's going to continue, probably get worse. I guess there are too many of us. Even if we have lots of talents and enthusiasm and training it may not matter much in the long run. Is it any wonder that so many of us take to drugs and other 'diversions,' as you put it? Do you have any idea how many young people in this country are tempted by suicide, even? I've just

come from the student lounge in the Arts Building, where I read some
fresh graffiti: 'Maybe I'll kill myself tonight.' Talk about superfluous!
"Don't get me wrong," you added hurriedly, noticing, I suppose,
my worried frown. "I'm not giving you any indirect 'message.' I
mean, I'm nowhere near that kind of desperation. But a significant
percentage of my contemporaries seem to be. And they don't find
death alluring because it's a way to heaven, believe me, but only
because it's a way out of some hell, real or imagined. I think they rep-
resent the extreme edge, so to speak, of a generation or two that is
wondering: Does life have any worthwhile meaning?"

So now we could talk. And we did—for a couple of hours, I sup-
pose, perhaps more. Did it make any sense to you, what I said? Faced
by such questions, two hours is a very short time. And convincing
"answers" are hard to come by. Sometimes I think you're better at
getting me involved in your questions than I am at persuading you to
consider my answers! Anyway, when I went home that night I had to
put it down in writing—for myself, as much as for you.

"I Came That They Might Have Life"

First let me say something as emphatically as I can: I am entirely
convinced that "salvation" as presented in the Bible and in the best
traditions of Christian faith, does not mean being saved *from* our
mortality, our finitude, our human creatureliness; nor does it
mean being saved *for* an otherworldly state, immortality, heaven.
In fact, when salvation is understood in that way, it distorts the
whole Christian message—a message that is the strongest possible
affirmation of life, creaturely life. The words I've used as the head-
ing for all that I want to say in this piece are words attributed to
Jesus by the author of the Gospel according to John (10:10). Of
the four Gospels, John is often thought to be the most "otherworldly"; but these words, and the context in which they appear,
indicate that the author believed Jesus' most basic intention was to
enhance life—to save us *from* "death," understood symbolically

and not only literally; to save us *for* life. So in the passage from which those words are taken the author contrasts the false savior, who "destroys" and "kills," with the true savior, Jesus, who "came that they might have life, and have it abundantly."

How does it happen, then, that so much historic and present-day Christianity seems bound up with being rescued from our creaturely condition, our mortality, and from condemnation on account of our enormous guilt? That is the critical side of your question, and it is quite right that you should ask it. In attempting to answer it, I want you to know that I sympathize very much with your sense of dissatisfaction with "salvation" conceived of in those ways. At the same time, I'd like to help you, if I can, to understand *why* it came about, historically, that death and guilt were so prominent in the salvation language of Christendom. I would also like to suggest why that language is still used so much today, and why it is largely inappropriate. After that, I'll try to say how I think the "good news" of salvation or redemption or whatever we may want to call it can and does speak to us still today—that is, to a society in which people often feel (as you put it) "superfluous."

To begin with, let's ask ourselves: Why did salvation come to be so closely associated with dying and getting to heaven? With a little historical imagination, you shouldn't have difficulty answering that. Imagine yourself living, say, in the third or the ninth century of our common era. You are born, let's assume, into a family of working people, maybe even slaves or serfs. You aren't going to climb up the social ladder into some other class, because there isn't any social ladder: "upward mobility," as it is sometimes called, does not apply until the modern period. You can expect to live— how long? Twenty-five years, perhaps forty? Probably less, the life expectancy being what it was right into our own epoch. You will certainly experience a lot of hardship throughout your short life.

Poverty and sickness will never be far from your door. You will marry someone of your own class, probably not for love, and you will begin at once having children, most of whom will die in infancy. You will work terribly hard from morning until night, and you'll pray you won't get sick or lose a limb, because there is nothing like workers' compensation or welfare. Social safety nets and unions and human rights are centuries away. Your expectations of this life, therefore, are mainly negative ones: that you can get through it without too much pain.

Not incidentally, a great many of the earliest Christians lived under just such conditions, and of course the majority of human beings throughout history have never been far removed from such a scenario. So what is "salvation" likely to mean for people in those circumstances? For most it will likely mean . . . "heaven." Heaven as consolation for the sorrows and deprivations of earth. Heaven as the good destiny that can offset the bad destiny, the fate, that seems one's unavoidable lot here and now, with death on the near horizon.

In other words, the powerful and lasting connection of salvation with an afterlife is obviously related to two facts of common human experience: grave disappointment with this life, and a combined fear and fascination in the face of death. Those experiences are still with us, all of us. But in the past century or so (not more) a portion of earth's human population has found ways of minimizing these negative experiences, particularly the first—disappointment with life. Our longer life expectancy in the so-called First World, combined with all our life-enhancing educational, political, scientific, and technological discoveries, have made this life infinitely more attractive than it must have been for most of our ancestors, and is still today for millions of earth's people. So if we, you and I, find the idea of salvation as "getting to heaven" distasteful and off-putting, we should not feel superior or self-righteous about it. We too have been more conditioned by our historical circumstances than we are likely to think. If anything, we should only feel grateful that the easing of our physical, material

condition has given us an opportunity to explore more fully the
deeper side of what salvation might mean.

What about the other combination—guilt, and salvation as release
from the punishment we deserve on account of our sins? Again I'd
like to ask you what you think might be behind this approach, historically speaking. Imagine you are living now, not in the period of
the early church or the early middle ages, but in a somewhat later
time—between, say, the eleventh and the sixteenth centuries. You
have been born into the family of a peasant or small farmer, or
perhaps a little shopkeeper or a petty government official. With
the plague on the move,[1] or a host of lesser but still mortal diseases, the fear of an early death has by no means been eliminated.
But it has been softened a little, cushioned, so to speak, by the
commonly held belief in an afterlife that could be radiant. The
church, it would seem, has done its work very thoroughly: it has
practically banished, or sent underground, the old *pagan* kind of
preoccupation with death and fate. You have more choice in your
ultimate destiny now, if not in your earthly one.

Ah! But there's the problem. So thoroughly has the now-official
Christian religion buttressed the humanly longed-for dream of an
afterlife that (intentionally or not) it has fanned the flames of
another ancient anxiety of our race: "Maybe there really will be an
afterlife, but *what kind of an afterlife will it be . . . for me? . . . for
those I love?*" It could be heaven, but it could more easily be hell—
or something in between. It depends on the individual—on you:
what you've done, what you haven't done. And you, being personally sensitive as well as highly conditioned by the lurid lore in
which the afterlife is everywhere depicted, are probably very anxious. You see your life being weighed in the balances and found
wanting. You feel oppressed by an evil you can't shake off. The
devil is a prominent feature of your spiritual environment. More-

over, since the guilt you have to bear is not only your own but the "original sin" by which your life has been tainted from the moment of conception, your fear of ultimate condemnation is very great—so great, perhaps, as to entice you to try to buy your way into heaven, as Martin Luther found some of his parishioners were doing, purchasing "indulgences" for themselves and their dear departed.

So why would you not think of the gospel of salvation in terms of the remission or pardoning of sin and guilt, mainly? And why would you not do everything in your power to have this assurance of divine pardon?

Has the sense of guilt disappeared from our society? Has the acceptability of so many different lifestyles, some of which were certainly regarded as hell-bent in the not-distant past, made us immune to guilt? You say you don't feel guilty, at least not as the most overpowering anxiety of your life, and I believe you. At the same time, I doubt if guilt has altogether disappeared. The psychotherapists and personal counselors would not be as busy as they are if it had. Guilt complexes and the restless search for acceptance are still with us; so is that deeper, mysterious, and unnameable sort of guilt that Franz Kafka and Søren Kierkegaard wrote about. And we aren't all that removed from the fear of death, either, what with cancer and AIDS and the appearance of new bacteria not susceptible to our antibiotics, and of course the rampant violence of our cities. These anxieties, as a great teacher of mine, Paul Tillich, taught us, belong to the human condition.[2] They are not likely to go away.

But—and this is where I think you are quite right—neither of these anxieties, neither death nor guilt, are what dominate the scene today. Not in our part of the world, at least. We've managed to soften the impact of mortality, partly by hiding it away in hospitals and mortuaries; and we've managed to "explain" our innate sense of guilt psychologically—indeed, so successfully that most people believe any sort of guilt feeling is an illness; and, in general, we've almost persuaded ourselves that anxiety *of any kind* is unnecessary and curable—with or without Prozac!

And yet . . . thinking people know perfectly well that that is untrue. An unanxious human being is a contradiction in terms, or a freak of nature, or maybe just lacking in self-knowledge! Of course people handle their anxieties differently—well or badly, creatively or neurotically. But to pretend we might have none, or grandly to announce that the future is going to be anxiety-free, is to fly in the face of all existing evidence. It is also, I'd say, to suggest that the human species really is on the decline. Because nothing noble or wise or worthy that human beings individually or collectively have ever done has been achieved in total absence of anxiety. To bring about the finally unanxious Homo sapiens would be to eliminate the "sapiens" from the "Homo."

On the other hand, who would want to pretend that human anxiety is, after all, just unambiguously beneficial, since so much goodness, beauty, and truth flows from it? Anxiety may goad us into inventiveness. It may lead us into depths of thought that we would otherwise never explore. It may even be necessary to the most profound experiences of love. But anxiety is also capable, in its excesses and without any counterforce, of making us apathetic, thoughtless, and repressive. Perennially anxious persons are often so bound up in themselves that they cannot even *see* those around them, let alone become real neighbors and friends to them. A whole society that is nursing some hidden anxiety can be a real menace in the world—especially if it is a powerful society, like ours. So let's not fool ourselves: being human, we certainly do need to be saved *from* something, and it's unlikely that any sort of cleverness on the part of our species is going to change that.

What does change, though, is the type—the character and shape, so to speak—of the anxieties that keep us from life, from living fully, "abundantly." And I think that you put your finger on the nature of the anxiety that typifies our historical and societal context today. What most Westerners need to be saved from today isn't dread of death, and it isn't a crippling sense of guilt—I agree. It's the gnawing suspicion that humans may be purposeless things, a species just as accidental as all the others—equipped, ironically enough, with all the attributes necessary to purposeful living, but in the end random, arbitrary, and . . . "superfluous."

Some critics would say that such an anxiety is superficial, a luxury anxiety of the affluent, something that people worry about when they've temporarily banished some of the *real* problems of life. But that's a shallow criticism, in my opinion. When people feel superfluous they are not only unhappy, they are frequently destructive. Precisely because human beings can be so talented and capable, they easily become frustrated and angry when they cannot find goals big enough for their capabilities. A good deal of the violence in our own society has been traced to unemployment and underemployment. People without work, or whose work is routine and meaningless to them, very often feel that their whole existence is without any purpose. Not infrequently they take out their profound frustration on those around them. There is no more horrendous scenario for the human future than one in which only a few human beings have any meaningful vocation— and that is a scenario entertained by many serious scholars today. So, anxiety about goals, purpose, meaning is by no means a luxury anxiety. It is probably the most critical anxiety of them all.

In fact, sometimes I think that history, paradoxically enough, has saved the worst human anxiety for our own period—for a time of greatest scientific and technological achievement. According to the Gospels, Jesus referred once to a man who had cleared his house of an "unclean spirit," only to expose it seven more demons far worse than the original one (Luke 11:24-26). Western civilization has taught us how to keep death somewhat at bay, or seem to, and how to handle guilt, or seem to. But in doing so it has made room for the still-more unnerving anxiety: the temptation to suspect that the whole enterprise called life, or history, may be (as that strangely contemporary man, William Shakespeare, put it) "a tale told by an idiot, full of sound and fury, signifying nothing."

The anxiety of purposelessness has always been present—read the Tower of Babel story in Genesis 11, or the Book of Ecclesiastes with its "All is vanity." But if you are preoccupied by the immediate pain and deprivation of life and the prospect of early death, or by your obvious sin and its probably horrendous punishment, then you do not get so far as worrying about "the meaning of it all." In fact, fixation on death and on guilt, as the rituals of all religions show, assumes and supports an underlying belief in life's *meaningfulness*. These anxieties presuppose that life is full of purpose. They are anxieties just because they get in the way of the purpose that there is. In other words, the old anxieties of death and guilt were part of the structure of the premodern, religious world, a world shot through and through with meaning.

By comparison, when the modern West swept its house clean of the old devils it swept the purposing gods out with them. With that bold housecleaning, we boasted at first that we ourselves were now at last "masters in our own house." But soon we discovered— or some of us did—that we weren't very adept at mastery, in fact. The whole modern historical exercise, from the French Revolution to the capitulation of Communism, has left us pretty bewildered. Clearly, humans are unusual creatures—but unusually destructive as well as unusually inventive. What does our braininess matter if, in the long run, it could be the source of our own and perhaps our planet's obliteration? So what precisely (as we may ask with Wendell Berry and others) "are human beings *for*?" If we are not just accidents of nature, what is our place in the scheme of things? What is our purpose and how could we attain it, or reclaim it?

What if we were to tackle the question of "salvation" with that kind of concern in mind? I know that we haven't done that very often or very imaginatively, we Christians. The so-called "conservative" Christians in our midst, who use the sin-and-salvation language most, have got stuck in the anxieties and salvation theories of the past; and the so-called "liberal" Christians, perhaps in some kind of adolescent reaction to the conservatives, tend to leave the whole idea of radical salvation alone, or else they reduce it to sentimental talk about God's love and forgiveness.

Personally, I am with the liberals in their refusal to use the heaven-and-hell approach of the conservatives, and in their refusal, also, to present Jesus as the innocent victim God needs in order to forgive the guilty. Along with many others throughout Christian history, I find that a ghastly misrepresentation of God. In fact, liberal critics may be right when they say that the whole language of salvation has been spoiled by crass, vulgar, and simplistic uses of it. On the other hand, I am with the conservatives when they assume that the human condition is one that needs radically to be "saved." When the Christian message is reduced to spiritual platitudes about love and forgiveness and hope and so on, the only people it can appeal to are people who haven't experienced the depths of human anguish and need—which may be why so much liberal Christianity is a very middle-class affair. I can't imagine why anyone would become really serious about this faith (or, indeed, about any religious faith whatsoever!) unless they felt that it spoke to their deepest need, their greatest anxiety. If "salvation," by whatever name, is less than radical—that is, if it doesn't reach down to the very roots (*radix*) of one's being—then why bother with it in the first place? Pep talks and "encouraging words" you can get from *Reader's Digest*. In refusing or neglecting to tackle the truly *basic* questions of human existence, most liberal Christianity on this continent is just digging its own grave.

I take it, then, that the question of whether life has any meaning *is* "basic." In fact, I'd say it's *the* basic question, because unless you can find some hint of an affirmative answer to that question all the other big questions are left hanging in midair—like, "What is truth?" What does it matter what "truth" is, or whether it can be had, or how it is to be distinguished from falsehood, and so forth, if a huge question mark is written over the whole project of life and history, including the meaningfulness of looking for truth? Or, "What is good?" If you are hung up on whether there is any purpose in all our striving, why would you give yourself heart and soul to asking this basic ethical question, about goodness? If in the end the good and the bad, as the world reckons them, are all reduced to dust and ashes, period, why exercise oneself about ethics? (That's not a theoretical question, by the way. One could legitimately ask why so much so-called ethical debate today has been reduced to talk about "values." Isn't it because we've concluded, as a society, that there is no good apart from our valuing—a valuing that becomes increasingly arbitrary: morality by consensus?)

So I accept the conclusion you yourself were led to in our discussion: that the great, overarching, undergirding question by which most people in our context are grasped is the question of meaning, or purpose, or vocation ("What are people *for*?"). One of the noblest spirits of our century, Dag Hammarskjöld, Secretary-General of the United Nations, spoke for his age when he wrote these words in his journal:

> What I ask for is absurd: that life shall have a meaning.
>
> What I strive for is impossible: that my life shall acquire a meaning.
>
> I dare not believe, I do not see how I shall ever be able to believe: that I am not alone.[3]

By the way, please remember for future reference the strange juxtaposition Hammarskjöld makes here between meaning and "being alone."

Not everybody *feels* the anxiety of meaninglessness as profoundly as Hammarskjöld, of course. There are degrees and shadings and stages of awareness of, and concern about, all that. But I agree that it is there, it is in the air, figuratively—well, almost literally, considering our ecological precariousness! It is at least as much *our* typical anxiety as fate and death were the anxieties of the ancients and guilt and condemnation the anxiety of our medieval forebears. The question for Christians is therefore, How does the Christian message speak to this anxiety? How does it liberate us from that debilitating kind of self-concern? How are people in our situation given life "more abundantly" through faith in the God who is made real and concrete to us through Jesus? Or—asking the same question in another way—how could Jesus become Christ for us—our "Messiah," our "Deliverer," our "Savior," the longed-for response to our deepest yearning?

How could Jesus become Christ for us?

I want to try to answer this (insofar as it can be answered in a general way, a way that could have a broad application even though it cannot speak to particular, individual lives) in two stages—but try to keep in mind that in actual experience the two are one, part of the same experience.

First, I think it would be impossible to find Jesus such a "liberator" unless one could feel that Jesus participated in the enslaving or oppressive realities from which one needed to be liberated. Just think about this for a moment in terms of ordinary human experience. You've likely had acquaintances who, when you had come up against some problem in your life, were all too ready to give you advice. From the heights of their relatively problemless life, they were reaching down, as it were, to give you a hand. It was very well intended. But it meant little to you, because in their presence you were conscious of one thing in particular: they were not "in your shoes." Their advice cost them little, and what it did for you more than anything else was to make you realize how far you were from their kind of carefree existence.

But then it may have happened (sometimes it really does) that someone came along who could actually understand your problem—from inside it, so to speak. This person wasn't condescending to you, she or he was on your level. Not in your shoes exactly, but on the same ground. You could talk. You felt you were understood. What you received from him or her was not just sympathy, but empathy, solidarity—a real *identification* with you in your dilemma.

You brought up "the incarnation" in one of our earlier discussions. Along with "the Trinity" and other bits of Christian doctrine, you said it was one of the things that got in the way for you. To some extent, I hope, I explained what "incarnation" means when I wrote last time about Jesus as the one who makes *particular* and *concrete*, for Christians, the thing that God wants most to communicate to us—God's own "Word," to use the biblical language (John 1:1ff.). But now at this point, in connection with our discussion of "salvation," I need to add something to that which I think is extremely important:

The incarnation doesn't just mean God showing us what God is like, or telling us through a life what God's living Word to us is. Beyond that, the incarnation means God's *participation* in our life, God's *identification* with us, God's *sharing* our creaturely condition, our "flesh." The God of the Jewish and Christian Scriptures is a God who yearns for us, like a parent for his or her lost child; a God who feels utter compassion for us—who, as the Bible puts us, "knows our frame, remembers that we are dust" (Ps. 103:14). Such a God—as anyone familiar with the older Testament would already have to realize—cannot just remain "God," up there, out there, far away. Such a God knows that there can be no solution to the problem of anxious humanity apart from God's becoming Personally involved, if I may put it that way. Unlike the friends who try to help you from the heights of their well-being, this God must become the friend who stands on the same ground with you, who knows your "frame" from inside of it. And when the newer Testament declares that God has indeed, in Jesus, "taken our flesh upon him," it is only carrying to its logical and even necessary conclusion the longing of the God who is already well known by the Jewish lawgivers and prophets. The incarnation became an abomination to Judaism, I think, only because the Christians, instead of interpreting it in those biblical terms, turned it into something strange like trying to mix oil and water, "divinity" and "humanity," in one life.

My point here is just this: the first stage in recognizing Jesus as "Savior" (liberator, rescuer, deliverer, Messiah, Christ) is recognizing him as one who is there *with you,* where you are, in all the particularity of your life. That is why the newer Testament calls him "Emmanuel," God-with-us.

But now we have to remember where *we* are—what *our* problem, *our* predicament is. And we've said that, so far as our overall situation in these relatively affluent Western societies is concerned, the problem is that we've become anxious about this very basic thing, whether there is any purpose in life and history. So we have to ask, "Can Jesus—as he is presented in the Gospels and epistles, as he is discussed in the most gripping traditions of the faith, as he is revealed among us in the Christian community—can this Jesus be said to *participate* in our kind of life, our anxiety? Could Jesus empathize with *us?*"

The answer that may first occur to anyone who has listened to Christian presentations of Jesus that are all too typical would probably have to be *no.* The "Jesus" of the televangelists, for instance, is usually so "divine," so powerful, so perfect that he is far more like your problemless friends than like the one who stands alongside you. And, to be honest, that kind of representation of Jesus, whether in the extravagant language of popular evangelism or the more polite humanistic talk of middle-class Christianity, is unfortunately pretty consistent with what has occurred throughout the history of Christendom. For reasons that are too complex to go into here, many Christians seem to think that if we don't present Jesus as "a winner" (to use language you introduced earlier) we'll limit his appeal. So the tendency throughout Christian history, with a very few notable exceptions, has been to color Jesus perfect, as it were: perfect in god-hood, perfect in man-hood. Yes, with the emphasis on "man," since to explore what some would call his "feminine side" would seem to many to diminish the things we've wanted most to emphasize about him—his great strength of personality, his singleminded uprightness, his power over his enemies, the steadfastness and competitiveness of his mission, his bold and defiant courage in the face of death, and so on. It would be hard to imagine such a Jesus wracked by self-doubt or, like Hamlet, torn by anxious thoughts about the legitimacy or truth or meaningfulness of his calling.

And in precisely that way, you see, we (I mean Christians collectively) have tended to undo the very thing that the word *incarnation* is meant to affirm: We've pushed Jesus back up into the heights, where he can only speak to us from way above our heads, if at all. In fact, so remote did much church doctrine and practice make Jesus appear, that a whole vast array of intermediary saints had to evolve in order that people could feel a little nearer to some flesh-and-blood representation of divine closeness and compassion. For of course the truth is that we human beings *are* flesh-and-blood, *are* frail and impermanent, *are* "down here," *are* or become—in one way or another, at one time or another—"losers." And so a "winner" deity or would-be savior, perfect in every way but especially in power, can only do for us what models of triumph always do, that is, make us even more conscious of our own weakness and absurdity.

But what if our picture of Jesus is really guided by what the biblical eyewitnesses say of him?[24] Whenever in Christian history there's been a genuine return to the Bible—and I am thinking especially of the Reformation, or some parts of it—there's also been a transformation of the church's image of Jesus: Instead of the powerful Jesus of established religion, people have learned once more something of the Jesus who had to live outside the establishment and was a victim of the powerful. Instead of the morally righteous Jesus of ecclesiastical law and order, the Jesus who all-too-jubilantly separates the sheep from the goats, people have encountered once again the Jesus who associated with "sinners" and found the "good" people proud and insufferable. Instead of the steadfast Jesus of pietism who is above every temptation, every emotion, every personal urge, ambition, and fear, people have discovered again the Jesus who is tempted almost beyond endurance, there in the wilderness, and who grows angry, and becomes exhausted, and is afraid. Instead of a Jesus full of unshakable faith in God and absolutely sure of his vocation and above every kind of doubt and anxiety, people encountering again the biblical Jesus discover one who can understand their own great uncertainties—one who, in fact, has probably gone much farther than they have into the dark night of doubt and despair; one who feels abandoned, not only by his friends and erstwhile followers, but by God—by the very God by whom he believes he has been sent, whose mission he thought he had been called to undertake in the world.

That Jesus, the crucified one, *is* able to empathize with us as members of a society that has lost its way, as persons who wonder whether there *is* any "way"—any road that leads anywhere. *That* Jesus is no stranger to our kind of alienation, our anxiety. And I would like to say that *that* Jesus is not just a figment of the imagination, or the result of reading only some of the things that the Bible says about him. No, Jesus as one who truly participates in life, life *as we know it*, is the real Jesus. All the others are false shepherds, "thieves," as John says, who in offering us easy access to life's abundance are really robbing us of any salvation worthy of the name.

Of course the Gospels tell us more than that Jesus "suffered and was rejected," that he "was crucified dead and buried" and "descended into hell," as the Apostles' Creed summarizes his story. *Of course* they depict his great kindness, his wisdom, his true (but never maudlin or sentimental) piety, and his victory over temptation and death and the demonic. But there is only one "perfection" that newer Testament is *consistently* interested in telling us about, where Jesus is concerned, and that is his perfect love. "Greater love no one has, than that one should lay down his life for his friends" (John 15:13). All other possible and actual perfections pale before this one. Indeed, apart from this one perfection, the perfection of love, none of the others is of much account, in the end (1 Corinthians 13). And the thing about love—it's true of all real love—is that it has to be ready precisely to "lay down" (that is, to forfeit), all other "perfections" for the sake of the beloved. A lover who is most interested in perfecting his own potentialities—his physical or mental prowess, his moral sensibilities, his amicability and popularity with others, and so on—is a poor, and likely soon to be a failed, lover. The only way open to the one whose commanding vocation is love is the achievement of real proximity to the beloved—really to be *with* the other. And if the beloved is "down here," languishing in quiet despair over life's seeming purposelessness, wondering whether "people" are "for" anything at all, and in general feeling "superfluous," then the lover will have to come "down here," at whatever cost to himself. That, at any rate, is where the act of love must begin, and without it there will be no beginning.

And in all of its words and phrases, paragraphs and "books," what the newer Testament wants above all to say to us is only this: It has happened—"the most wonderful thing has happened."[5] At great cost, Love has come down to where we are. You are loved—and not only from afar, not only by Somebody "up there."

I said that there would have to be two stages in my answer to the question whether the gospel of Jesus as savior could also speak to those who suffer under "the anxiety of meaninglessness and despair," to use Paul Tillich's language. But I also added, you will remember, that the two stages are only for the purpose of talking about all this; in reality they are part of the one process of communication, the one experience. And now I can explain a little better what I meant by that addition.

For the truth is, surely, that those who feel themselves to be loved have already begun to experience the overcoming of their problem; because their "problem," whatever it is, is at bottom their feeling of isolation. They feel they are alone with their great burden. They find no response to their anxious questions from

Alone

beyond themselves. They sense they are living outside the communion of others, or that the others in whose company they live can neither understand nor share their condition. In their alienation and loneliness, they feel quite incapable of overcoming anything—of achieving the purpose and direction that they yearn for. Remember how Dag Hammarskjöld's poignant journal entry links the "absurd" and "impossible" quest for meaning with his sense of being "alone"?

The very presence of another who is able to share one's lot is at least the beginning of the resolution of one's predicament, whatever that predicament is concretely. This is undoubtedly why people almost universally and almost as a law of human relationships seek out others who suffer in ways similar to their own. And it is also why it has been found—in groups like Alcoholics Anonymous, for example, or victims of cancer, or abused women—that the discovery of others who can identify profoundly with one's suffering is already a source of comfort, even of joy, and often even of recovery.

It is not essentially different from these common experiences of human beings when Christians feel that in encountering the Spirit of Jesus they have been met by one who is truly "with" them and "for" them—and, usually, with and for them in ways that even their closest human associates cannot be expected to be. Already in sensing that their suffering is shared, that they are not alone, that they are not beyond companionship and help, they have begun the journey toward recovery and health.

There—I've introduced a word that I have been wanting to bring into this discussion all along: *health.* Do you know (most people don't, I find) that the word at the center of this whole discussion, "salvation," comes directly from the Latin word for "health"—*salus?* It means to be whole, to be integrated. You may think, for instance, of the way that Jesus in the Gospels, in healing someone of some debilitating illness, tells them, "Be whole."[6] Or you may think of something more mundane—such as that when we "salute" someone we are really wishing them health; or such as the 1960's expression of "getting it together," which means over-coming fragmentation, achieving greater personal integration. All that kind of thing lies behind the word that we too often turn into something so "spiritual," religious, and "otherworldly" that it betrays the most fundamental meaning of the word itself, which is a very earthy thing: the healing of persons, the reintegrating of divided selves, the reuniting of people with those from whom they are estranged, equipping us for the kind of life our Creator intend-ed us to have. "I came that they might have life and have it more abundantly."

But now we have to notice something very important: this "way" toward life, this "beginning" that is made whenever a human being feels befriended by the God whom Jesus makes present—it is not to be understood as if the journey were already completed, or as if the beginning were already an ending. Just a moment ago I referred again to the contrast that John's Gospel makes between the authentic and the false savior, whom Jesus calls the thief. This is no ordinary thief, easily recognizable as such. This thief is a real "con artist." He seems to be offering us a wonderful "deal"—Get rich quick! Get life right away! New lives for old!

That, unfortunately, is just how Christian "salvation" is fre-quently pedaled by hucksters of religion in our midst today. As if, whatever one's anxiety, one could exchange it immediately for its opposite, its sure cure: for death, life; for guilt, pardon; for despair, hope. The false savior goes in for immediate remedies to every conceivable problem—like medical quacks who promise instant cures. "Salvation" of this sort is not only a cruel trick, for it is illu-sory; it is also cheap and shallow—so shallow, in fact, that it gives the whole Christian understanding of salvation a very bad name, putting it for many of our contemporaries into the same category as quackery and false advertising.

I said that the experience of God's presence with us, in the Incarnate One, is a beginning, the first step toward *salus*—wholeness. But it is only a beginning. We should not be surprised if, accompanied by *this* shepherd, we are led—not into immediate light and all things positive, but into what must seem to us, at first, even greater darkness. But our surprise, if we go far enough along this path, will eventually be qualified by a certain understanding of the journey into darkness. There are reasons for this—yes, once again, there are reasons!

The most obvious reason has already been hinted at: to receive anything deserving of the term *wholeness* we have to know the extent of our brokenness—what in traditional theological language is called "sin." To become really healthy we have to face the real causes of our illness, and not be satisfied with treating its symptoms or with quick fixes. Or, translating that into the language of anxiety that we used earlier: if our anxious fears are due to a suspicion that our life, and perhaps the whole phenomenon of creaturely life, is without purpose, then it will be necessary for us to explore that anxiety more deeply than just entertaining it as a vague feeling that gnaws away at us at the level of the subconscious or semiconscious. Why?

Because the object of this journey that we have begun in the company of the one who wants us to have *life* is that we should learn true *hope*, without which life is impossible. *True* hope, not false or cheap hope. Not the kind of hope that whistles in the dark, or even just at twilight! And true hope, as distinct from mere optimism, is given only to those who have had some profound exposure to hope's opposite—despair. It's easy to manufacture something that looks like hope if you have never descended into the depths, like the psalmist who writes, "Out of the depths have I cried unto thee" (Ps. 130:1). The world—our determinedly, officially "optimistic," North American world especially—is practically drowning in thousands of schemes and dreams that are the consequences of cheap hope. Real "salvation," as distinct from the illusory offers of "the thief," needs a hope that is not afraid to have

Jesus offers not immunity — but Companionship

dialogue with despair. What Jesus as savior offers us is not immunity from despair, any more than it is immunity from any other form of human doubt, but his companionship in the dark night. He has been there. He knows the way. He knows that the darkness is not all there is, and that even at its blackest *the darkness itself holds purpose.* For without it we cannot distinguish the light, any more than we can distinguish true hope without brushing into despair, or true forgiveness without going still deeper into our guilt (Kafka!), or true, "abundant" life without a close encounter with death in its many guises.

But there is another, perhaps less obvious reason why this way toward light and hope and forgiveness and life has to pass through the antitheses of all these (and not just once, but time and again)—another reason why it is rightly called "the way of the cross." And it is this: It is the will of *this* savior, not only that we should *personally* experience hope, forgiveness, life, and all such positive things in a truly genuine way, but that in the process of this discovery we should come to know others who need this "abundance"—and especially those whose need is greater than our own. The God of the Bible is not interested in saving individual souls alone! It is *the whole* that this God wants to make whole; the entire creation, disintegrating under the impact of human anxiety and grasping, must be reintegrated. And so much is this the case that there is really no kind of *individual* wholeness that can be brought to completion apart from the salvation of the whole. The *salus* for which the God of the Jewish and Christian Scriptures yearns is the integrating of the whole creation, the reconciling of humans not only with God but also with one another and with the nonhuman creatures—yes, with the earth itself.

And let us be very honest: We especially who live in this rather favored place, whose material, educational, medical, and other immediate worries are on the whole soothed by economics; whose anxieties, though terrible enough to ourselves and even unbearable often, are by comparison with millions of our contemporaries less than abysmal; whose consciousness of human need and of the "groaning of the whole creation" (as Paul says in Romans 8:22) is, with exceptions, all too superficial: Isn't it likely that such people as we are would on our own achieve very little by way of solidarity with our fellow creatures, human and extrahuman, unless we were carried—probably against our will!—into the darkness where much of humanity actually lives? And isn't it in fact likely that we would be far happier with a "salvation" that gives us personal "peace of mind"?

But that, you see, is not "salvation" in biblical terms. For the love that sends God's Representative away from the realm of the eternal into the "far country" of time is a love directed, as that same Gospel of John insists, toward "the world"—the *cosmos* (John 3:16). It is not interested in snatching a few souls from the world's burning and carrying them off to "heaven." It wants to redeem the whole lost creation—it is that ambitious for wholeness, *salus*.

So . . . those who feel themselves to be undeserving recipients of this *agape*, this "suffering love" of the God made known through the life of Jesus, know that they must enter even more deeply into the darkness of this world than they would otherwise have done. And the reason is not only that they should learn to distinguish true from false claims of salvation but that, in the process of their own exposure to the world's darkness, they should meet and befriend the others who live in that darkness. The light toward which they move will be real light, even if it is only as bright as a candle, only if in the process of passing through the darkness they have joined hands with others whom they are bound to encounter there.

And when, one of these days, we have the opportunity of talking about "the church," I hope you will remember this image of mine.

For now, though, let me conclude: There is of course no definitive "conclusion" to our understanding of salvation; for in the end it always hinges on the specifics of life and history—the life and history of communities, the lives and histories of individuals. The key question is always the one that you stated when you asked, "What do we need to be saved *from*?" And the answer to that question will always depend on who "we" are, precisely—corporately, personally.

Following your own lead, I have assumed here that, *corporately* speaking, "we" who belong to this so-called First World context, need to be saved from the anxiety of being without purpose or meaningful vocation; and so I have tried to show that what "we" are saved *for* is the vocation of friendship, solidarity, and the stewardly care of others. There can be no more significant purpose and vocation than that, as everyone knows who begins to find himself or herself beckoned into that calling.

But of course salvation cannot be restricted to those who suffer under the burden of meaninglessness. There are those still who feel overpowered by the fear of death and the afflictions of this life—and indeed, at some points in our lives, that anxiety grasps all of us. And there are those, too, who are prevented from abundance of life by their consciousness of their own guilt—and this, too, is an anxiety to which any of us can easily be subjected. The point, however, is just this: *whatever* stands in the way of our full entry into life in all of its admixture of joy and sorrow, that is the "sin" from which we must be saved. For the purpose of this savior is to give us *life*, abundant life, the life that the Creator God intended for us from the outset—life that is "very good" (Genesis 1).

Jesus, for Christians, stands at the center of God's labor for creation's salvation because, as Dorothy Sayers once put it, God was not content to call creation good from a distance.

. . . But How?

four

*You arrived a little early today. The frown on your forehead suggest-
ed to me that you had come to a certain impasse in your thoughts
about Christianity. Your words soon confirmed that impression. I
knew that we were in for a long session.*

"I'm grateful to you for taking the trouble to write such a lengthy
and careful statement about salvation," you began; "In fact, it's very
generous of you to treat my questions so seriously. I didn't realize this
when we began to have these chats, but I know now we're thinking
about really complicated things. So I don't want you to feel that I
expect you to give me the kinds of answers I'd get, maybe, if I were
talking to someone about mathematics, or physics, or even history.
One has to talk around questions like these—and probably over a
long period of time. In another sense, though, just talking around
them is already a way of beginning to come to terms with them—
emphasis on beginning, of course. I mean, the fact that we can do
this—can actually communicate with one another about these questions—is itself . . . well, it's something, *don't you think?*"

I did. "I often wonder, in fact," I said, "whether the only 'answers'
that matter, where these kinds of questions are concerned, are the
ones that people are sometimes able to glimpse as they reflect on them
together."

"That's an interesting thought," you replied. "I'll remember that. . . . Anyway, I wanted to say that to you—to thank you, I mean— because . . . well, to be frank, there's something that has been bothering me. I'm almost afraid that if I bring it up it will make you think you are wasting your time with me."

Now I was really curious. What could this subject be that had made you so hesitant to introduce it? Were you about to become very personal, confess something—perhaps, despite your protestations of having no feelings of guilt, blurt out some guilty secret? It had happened to me before. So I tried to look as nonjudgmental as I could.

"Let me put it this way," you began. "I can follow nearly everything you say, both in our discussions and in your little essays afterward. I understand it, nearly always, even when it doesn't quite mesh with my own assumptions and experiences. But that's where it stops—with 'understanding.' I mean, I follow the argument, usually. I can see the sense in it. Your 'reasons' do, most of them, explain a lot. . . ."

Here I felt I might interrupt briefly. I said: "You know this word understanding is a fascinating word. Literally, it means to 'stand under.' Like standing under something you can see in part, but not being able to see the whole of it. It means that real understanding is never—well, it's never 'understanding' in the way we usually use that word. There's always a large element of unknownness in it, because the thing you are trying to understand is bigger than you are."

"That's just it!" you exclaimed. "I can understand enough of all this to know that I don't understand it! I can't grasp hold of it. I can't get inside it. I feel like an outsider most of the time, in fact. I can see why you would want to think in the way that you do, usually, but even when I try hard to make your reasoning my own, it just doesn't come off.

"For instance," you went on, "when you wrote about Jesus as being like a friend who stands on my own ground, where I am, unlike the friends who talk down to me from their heights—well, I like that idea, of course. Who wouldn't be grateful for such a friend? But for the life of me I can't feel that Jesus is anywhere near me, let alone right 'down here' with me!

"Do you see what I mean? Jesus is back there in history, nearly two thousand years back. Christians talk about him all the time as if he were just next door, or even closer! I don't know how they can do this. At the same time, I can see that this—this sense of his presence, or whatever—is vital to them. To you, too. Without that, your 'reasons,' I think, would lack any foundation in experience. Obviously you aren't one of these people who go around sensing unseen 'presences' all over the place. You seem to have your feet on the ground. But what did you mean, in your last piece, when you spoke about the 'Spirit of Jesus'? How do late-twentieth-century people like us, products of the age of science, acquire enough of a sense of mystery to make us open to such 'spirit' talk without cutting us off altogether from our own world and its assumptions?"

My mind was racing. Where to start, what to say? In your great and typical honesty you had once again dragged another kind of spirit—the Spirit of the Age, the Age of Fact and Verifiability and Know-How—into my quiet study, and awakened once again, in me, the sleeping giant of doubt. I could only hope that this giant might in turn be challenged by something greater, however fragile my grasp of it. For many reasons, not all of them intellectual, I found myself remembering the words of an ancient Christian hymn: "Come, Holy Spirit."

Secularism, Spirituality, and the Holy Spirit

What you are asking about (forgive me, I was almost tempted to say what you are asking *for*) is what Christian tradition refers to as "the Holy Spirit." That's what your "How?" is all about. In fact, in an odd sort of way your question, even down to some of the language you use, is reminiscent of many of the conversations between Jesus and his disciples that are recorded in the Gospels. These disciples too, ordinary people not given to flights of fantasy or mystical visions, are constantly baffled by the things that Jesus says and does. They understand, yet they also do *not* understand. His parables—those seemingly simple, illustrative stories—obviously intrigue them, but frequently they miss their point altogether. Sometimes they grasp bits and pieces of his teachings, and are moved by some of the things that he says and does; nevertheless, they give expression again and again to a typical frustration: they know, it would seem, that they are missing something, and that this something is not just incidental, but is the key to everything else.

Perhaps because it was written later than the other Gospels, John's Gospel confronts this problem in a quite explicit way. Midway through his account (John 13–16), this author introduces a scene that rather epitomizes the frustration of the disciples in their wanderings with their teacher. All along, the poor fellows must have wondered where these meanderings were taking them, and now the impulsive Peter puts the question to Jesus directly and even bluntly: "Lord, *where are you going?*"

I find it a lovely thing to see this question right there in the middle of the story. We romanticize the apostles if we imagine that they simply followed Jesus unquestioningly. Many of his followers, we know, left him. The Twelve stayed on—"To whom else would we go?" they asked. But always there was this gnawing doubt about the aim of the whole enterprise: "Lord, precisely where are you taking us?"

Jesus replies, enigmatically enough, that they "cannot follow where he is going." This aggravates their uncertainty even more, for they hear the answer (as the author of John obviously intended it) as a reference to Jesus' approaching death. Does not this death, which is predictable enough given his deteriorating relations with both secular and religious authorities, spell the end of everything for them? And in that case, what purpose has been served by their following him—and at such cost to themselves and their families?

Then Jesus, sensing their confusion and feelings of abandonment, introduces our theme: the promise of the divine Spirit: "'I will not leave you orphaned; I am coming to you. . . . the Advocate, the Holy Spirit, whom the Father will send in my name, will teach you everything, and remind you of all that I have said to you.'" And later he adds: "'I still have many things to say to you, but you cannot bear them now. When the Spirit of truth comes, he will guide you into all the truth; for he will not speak on his own, but will speak whatever he hears.'"

The assumption here, and indeed throughout the newer Testament, is that the life and mission of Jesus, while in a certain sense it will be completed with his death (he himself on the cross announces that "It is finished"), in another way only *begins* at that ending. The termination that is Jesus' crucifixion is understood by the newer Testament as what in Latin is called a *terminus a quo*— not an end *to* which (*ad quem*) everything moves, but an end *from* which (*a quo*) something now takes place—something new. In their wanderings with their unofficial "Rabbi," the disciples are already being prepared for that new possibility, though they don't rightly know it. Even their confusion and frustration seem to be necessary to what is to happen later. They must taste the experience of being baffled and bumbling, empty of answers, before they can gain a depth of (yes) *understanding* that surpasses their present mixture of knowing and not-knowing. Right up until the coming of the Holy Spirit, described in Acts 2, these close followers of Jesus, the very "inner circle" of his disciples, feel like "outsiders"—that was your word, and it is just the right one. Though they are on the inside, so far as physical proximity to Jesus is concerned, they know they are still outsiders. Some vital connection is missing.

What is this missing "ingredient," according to the Scriptures? What is it that can only be supplied by the Spirit of God—that even Jesus himself, while physically present among them, cannot give them? To answer that, we must use several biblical and theological concepts:

- *metanoia*: a change of heart and direction, an about-face, repentance, conversion; external change is not enough; the change that is necessary, if the outsiders are to become insiders, is an internal change, a changed spirit;

- *enlightenment*: the gift of inward illumination, the experience of truly comprehending what before could only be heard "with the hearing of the ears," to use a biblical expression; this is what Jesus meant by saying that the Spirit would lead his disciples into truth, truth that they could not "bear" just now;

- *faith*: far from merely imparting knowledge, it is the work of the divine Spirit to awaken in them a response of trust—trust in the God who has been made known to them through Jesus;

- *calling*: the effect of the change (*metanoia*) that comes over them, deepening their understanding and evoking their faith, is to give them a new and bold sense of their vocation, their mission; they are not changed, enlightened, and enabled to trust God just for their own *salus* (salvation); they are *sent out* into the world by this personal experience—because, as I said before, it is the world that God wants to redeem, not just individual persons, and not just "the church." This is why the very first act of the disciples following the Pentecost experience (that is, the coming of the Holy Spirit), is public preaching of the "Good News."

Now, in all of this we encounter a dimension of Christian faith so important that one would have to say that, without it, there would have been no such thing as Christianity, and we wouldn't have been discussing any of this. For, while Jesus (as we've already observed) is at the very center of this faith, he alone, as a historical figure, could not have brought about the response that was needed to inaugurate and sustain an enduring community of faith.

In other words, it is not really adequate or right to think of Jesus only as the historic "founder" of Christianity, as he is sometimes designated—as if, like the founder of a philosophic school or political movement, he had got the movement going, and then it became self-perpetuating. That Jesus was the "founder" of Christianity may of course be said, but it is not a sufficient explanation of the Christian faith, and for reasons closely related to the problem with which you introduced this discussion. There must be some sense, on the part of such a community, that their "founder" is still present with them, guiding, enabling, judging, sustaining them.

What ordinary founders of movements *can* do, Jesus also did, and much more thoroughly than most founding personalities: that is, through his teaching, his healings, his relationships, and above all the conduct of his own life and death, he established the model of "the Way" that he intended his followers to go. They would subsequently have constantly to refer themselves and their teachings and behavior in the world to that model, to test the authenticity of their own life and work.

But there is something that founders *cannot* do, though they all attempt it—something that Jesus also, as founder of the Christian "Way," could not do so long as he intended (as he clearly did) to remain within the bounds of strictly human possibilities and not resort to suprahuman or divine power. I mean that founders, including Jesus, are not able to bring about profound *internal* transformations within the secret and innermost spirits of their followers. While with their persuasive teachings and charismatic personalities founding figures like Socrates or Karl Marx may come very close to effecting deep personal convictions in their immediate circle of disciples, they cannot transform the inner selves of the persons who surround and succeed them; and with the founders' deaths and the swift passage of the years the remembrance of their presence ceases to have even the degree of influence they had in their lifetimes. Soon, as we know from the history of both the Socratic and the Marxist schools of thought, among many others, there occur serious divisions in the once-quite-united movements, brought on by new interpretations and new leaders; and soon, too, the lively discourse of the founder is reduced to doctrines and systems and slogans to which allegiance is demanded, often, in a way that would have shocked the founders themselves.

The transforming truth to which Jesus wanted to introduce his disciples, the truth he names in the passage quoted above, truth that both convicts and liberates—such truth could not and cannot be reduced to dogmas, propositions, and systems that can be written down, memorized, and regurgitated. When this happens, it is no longer the lively, life-altering truth that was originally intended. Truth, if it is gripping enough to deserve that high name, always transcends "truths." Such truth must always emerge out of its unpossessible, living source, and it can only be received by human beings who themselves are made ready and willing to hear and be changed by it.

The truth into which Jesus intends his disciples to be "led" by the "Comforter" whom he promises to send, is just this *living truth*, which, in order to achieve a foothold in the lives of those who hear it, must radically alter those lives. For theirs (and ours!) are lives that manifest an abiding resistance to truth. Truth makes all human beings uncomfortable; it calls us into question; it makes demands of us that are beyond our ordinary capacities, not to speak of our habitual intentions and preferences. As the historical Jesus (according to John) told his original disciples, the way of truth to which he wished to initiate them could not be borne by them "just yet." First their innermost selves—their minds, hearts, souls, spirits—must be made ready to receive it. And that would be the work of "the Comforter," the divine Spirit.

What we are encountering in this whole discussion is a dimension of Christian experience that has been hard for many modern Westerners to grasp. One meets this dimension everywhere in Christian tradition, and indeed (in different ways) in all religious traditions, but it becomes unavoidable and central in Christian teaching concerning the Holy Spirit. What shall we call this dimension? We could call it the "transcendental" dimension, meaning that it goes beyond or transcends what we as modern Western people consider ordinary experience of the world. Or we could call it the mystical dimension, because it assumes the possibility of encountering mysteries not accessible to the usual processes of knowing, and of experiencing relationship with presences invisible to sensory perception. Or we could call it, simply, the spiritual dimension, referring by this to a communion of the human spirit with a center of consciousness, being and willing that is not present to us in an obvious, material form, though it is altogether real.

I say that this dimension, without which Christianity (and most if not all other religious faiths) would not exist, has been very hard for modern Westerners to grasp or to take seriously. Of course, it doesn't help matters that so much of the most vocal "spiritualism" we have observed in and around our very secular environment, much of it avowedly "Christian," has been so unacceptable to sane and sober minds. Often it has appeared simply bizarre, or even ridiculous. But even more subdued and nonostentatious forms of spirituality seem foreign to the secular mentality. Perhaps enlightened, tolerant persons are willing to listen to ancient or even contemporary "mystics" as if they were poets or dreamers; but the general effect of two or more centuries of sensory-based (empirical) rationality has made most of us skeptical of any religious or even quasi-religious thought that assumes the reality of presences or influences or relationships that cannot be explained by reference to data that is subject to "scientific" (that is, empirical and controlled) investigation.

Even if "the modern mind" admits that there is much that we do not understand, and in that sense admits of "mystery," such a mind is likely to consider the unknown simply as that which *still remains to be known*, rather than as being permanently beyond our usual means of measurement. While possessors of such a mentality are usually tolerant of those who claim to have knowledge of God or to be in communion with the risen, living Christ through the mediation of the Holy Spirit and so forth, they harbor a strong suspicion of all such claims. Such claims are so completely inconsistent with the fact-oriented world of our daily experience as a people that when they are not regarded with open skepticism they are usually politely relegated to the realm of "religion"—a realm which may or may not be respected, depending on differing social circumstances.

You yourself were giving expression to this secular bias of the modern Western mind when you said that while you could "understand," at a certain degree of comprehension, what I said and wrote about Jesus and his centrality to Christian faith, you could not grasp what Christians mean when they speak of Jesus as one who is present to them here and now. In what I have said just now about the Holy Spirit, I hope that I have at least pointed to what Christians mean when they speak of the presence of the God made particular and concrete for them through Jesus, and so of Jesus' own presence to them. But I know perfectly well that this explanation, so far as it goes, will not have cleared up the difficulty you feel. In fact, in a way, this discussion of the Holy Spirit may even have heightened that difficulty for you. For while, within the framework of modern secularity, it is certainly possible to speak about the influence of the historical Jesus, when it comes to belief in the work of the Holy Spirit the standards of knowledge accepted by the modern world seem to have been completely cast aside.

I do not think, to be honest, that I am ever going to produce any arguments—*as* arguments—that will overcome for you this difficulty (I mean this sense of your being "an outsider"). In fact, as I have already observed, the only thing that will alter your attitude to all of this is an inner transformation that neither I nor any other human being can cause to happen within you. You, too, could become the subject of a *metanoia*, though that is not mine to arrange. Nevertheless, if we continue to reflect on this subject at the level of "reasons"—reasons that cannot pretend to be proofs and do not wish to be thought so—it may be possible to clear the way for the divine Spirit to struggle with your spirit, as has happened with others before you—myself included. Who knows, perhaps the "understanding" that you already feel is the beginning of deeper kind of "standing under."

With that end in mind, let's think a little about something quite interesting that has been happening lately in this fact-obsessed Western world of ours. As you are certainly aware, during the past decade or so, a word has entered the common speech of people in our part of the world that, I can assure you, no one forty or fifty years ago would have thought to hear from us except in the realm of "religion"; and even there it was not frequently used. The word is *spirituality*. Now one hears this word everywhere, often in the most unlikely places. Sometimes it is linked with another catchword of the age, *values*: "There are spiritual values," an aspiring politician announces, "that must not be set aside in our fast-moving society." Even businesses and advertisers know how to employ this language—usually, to be sure, for crass economic purposes; but then, they wouldn't use the term at all unless they knew it had some appeal for their "target group." Whole movements have sprung up, some of them admittedly religious, but others wishing to stay clear of the turmoil and in-fighting of conventional religions, and some (like much "New Age" spirituality) pretending to be "postreligious." People discover that nature is in fact brimful of spirit, that rocks and trees and brooks—yes, even the planet itself, as in the Gaia theory promulgated first by James Lovelock—may be said to possess life and spirit. Suddenly there is an unheard-of interest in the spirituality of the indigenous peoples of this continent, and in Celtic spirituality, and other premodern approaches to the mystery of life.

In fact, many would link this search for transcendence and the new openness to mystery with postmodernism—a term that is still so variously defined as to its positive meaning that the only agreement about what it is is that it is *not* modernity, it is *post-modern*.

What is going on here? It is quite astonishing, if you've lived long enough to witness the enormous change it represents. Less than four decades ago, when I was just beginning my professional career as a theologian, all the "with-it" people (as we presumptuously dubbed ourselves then) in our liberal and moderate Protestant circles were reading and praising books written by Christian thinkers who wanted to celebrate secularity. We all thought it a marvelous thing that the Christian faith did not regard this world as "sacred," or steeped in such mystery that it must always elude our grasp. We realized, with a kind of relief, that as Christians we could accept and rejoice in the secularity of the world, seeing it as a "system" that was in some real way self-contained and self-perpetuating. We could take hold of our human responsibilities within this system—yes, certainly, our God expected us to "take charge" within the sphere of nature. Moreover, far from feeling that Christianity had been bypassed by secularism, we should recognize (so we felt) that it was precisely Christianity that gave birth to secularism; for the Christian doctrine of creation meant that the world is separate from God, and not to be endowed with any kind of divinity itself.

And now, in so short a time, all of this has come to seem very premature and questionable. Why? The reason, I think, is that

secularism went too far. Like most worldviews—most "isms"—
secularism has certain built-in weaknesses and dangers, and the
more it presses unchallenged toward its own full expression the
more obvious the weaknesses and dangers are seen to be. For one
thing, the tendency of secularism to dispel mystery and see everything as being ultimately fathomable and even controllable—this
has to be regarded, finally, as both a weakness and a danger.
Because everything just *isn't* understandable, and it certainly is
not all subject to human control; and when people start behaving
as if there were "no limits" to either their knowledge or their mastery, the results can be horrific. Nobody can, or ever will, tell us
from a strictly scientific point of view why there is something and
not nothing. Neither will human beings generally come to the
point of calmly accepting suffering and death just because they
are "natural."

Moreover, there seems to be a persistent need in us to have and
to nurture some sense of mystery. So many of our experiences—
including the most decisive and dramatic of them, like falling in
love, or mourning someone's passing, or being filled with inex-
pressible joy before some natural occurrence or work of art—are
so steeped in mystery that, without it, they would be robbed of
everything that gives them meaning.

Secularism also, it should be remembered, went hand in hand
with a certain economic and technological boom, following on the
public euphoria that occurred in the aftermath of World War II. It
is easy, and perhaps even predictable, in such periods of security
and optimism, for people to think that the world is going their way,
and that they themselves are beings of unusual accomplishment,
for whom no task is impossible. But, in the meantime, a great many
events and occurrences—the advent of nuclearism, Viet Nam, the
crisis of nature, the failure of so many of our institutions including
governments, economic slumps, joblessness, and other things
we've already touched on here and there—have conspired to make
us, as a people, far less confident of our own abilities as masters in
a world that is no longer so "user-friendly," that the secular bravado

of three or four decades ago has practically disappeared among us. I don't, of course, mean that secularism has come to an end. It is still a mighty factor in the global situation at large. But its heyday in North America has, I think, passed—and in certain parts of Europe, too. We went far enough along the secular way to find out its costs and its disappointments. For many of us, it is a god that failed, an illusion; as an "ism" it has lost its great appeal.

And that has left us open, in new ways, to . . . spirituality. One can notice a kind of pendulum swing here, can't one? If one goes far enough toward a materialistic worldview like secularism, one discovers the limits and false promises of that system—quite possibly one was personally hurt by the system's unacknowledged dangers, as so many in the former Marxist lands were. So it is somehow natural that one starts to swing back to the other side of the spectrum—which is some antimaterialistic outlook, some kind of spiritualism. One wants to correct things, at least to restore some balance. It's a matter of survival!—and not only personal, but social survival.

What should Christians think about this new openness to the realm of "spirit?" Well, in my opinion they should be both open to it and (what shall I say?) vigilant, watchful. Let me explain why—as briefly as I can:

First, Christians should be open to the new spirituality because it really is a corrective to so much that has influenced—and conspicuously harmed!—the modern world. Materialism of every kind, whether ideological communism or unrestrained capitalism, is simply one-sided, false, and humanly demeaning. Certainly we are "matter" and we live in a material environment; but if in our thinking everything is reduced to matter then very bad things soon begin to occur. Nature is "thingified," and we think we can do with it whatever we want. The result is pollution, the disappearance of species, the depletion of the ozone layer, global warming, and so on. Human beings too are turned into objects—after all, we're just part of matter. The personhood of persons no longer counts for anything. People become statistics, digits within a vast quantifiable whole. Finally the human spirit rebels against this reduction of itself; and Christians should see that rebellion as being "of God"!

What I am saying to you in this is that the fact-conscious, hard-data, and in that limited sense, "scientific" world that is suspicious of anything labeled "spiritual," is being profoundly challenged in our time. And the challenge is coming, not only from religiously committed people like me, but from every aspect of human consciousness, *including* much of the best science, which has never been as materialistic as secular ideologies make it out to be. You yourself, let me remind you, borrowed rather too heavily on the materialist-secularist point of view when you spoke so passionately about how absurd spiritual ideas like the continuing presence of Jesus are to the modern, scientific mentality. I am just reminding you (I think you already know it!) that this so-called modern, scientific mentality "ain't what it used to be." For it was all too uncritically bound up with that ideological secularism that was ready to use science for its own purposes, but was in fact very selective in its choice of the "science" it used.

In saying this, I don't want you to hear that I now believe it is perfectly easy and straightforward to believe in "spirit"— whether that means the Holy Spirit or the human spirit, or for that matter spirit as a dimension of nature itself. It is neither simple nor natural to do so. Christian faith, like every other *thinking* system of meaning, continues to struggle with the prospect that matter may be all there is—that what we see (feel, touch, taste, and smell!) is what we get! But at least you should realize that Christians are not alone today in confessing that there are realities, forces, or dimensions that cannot be analyzed by the usual processes of scientific investigation, though some far-seeing scientists themselves sense them; that these realities *are* nonetheless very real; and that their recognition on the part of human beings is vital not only to our understanding but to our very survival as a civilization.

Isn't the very fact that there *is* something and not nothing, when (and if!) you come to think of it, rather astonishing? Closer to home, is not your own being, including the mystery of your birth, the wondrous way in which all your "parts" form a more or less integrated "whole"; including also the ongoing drama and unpredictability of your development, your relationships, your loves, your hopes and fears—isn't all of this a wonder so saturated with mystery that the thought of a presence called "Holy Spirit" may not be such an immense leap for you as may at first appear? Especially when, all around you today, there are countless others, just as intelligent and often even more hard-nosed than you, who have found they must abandon their earlier, strictly one-dimensional points of view and realize that life is more than it appears, on the surface, to be?

But wait!—I am not saying this in order to push you into a belief for which you are not ready. That would be a foolish and even a wicked thing for me, or any other believing Christian, to attempt—though many do so. Only the Spirit of God is permitted to wrestle with your spirit in that way, because your personhood may not be violated or your freedom abused. Only the divine Spirit, the Spirit by whom we were created, can enter into such a destiny-filled dialogue with the human spirit honorably—that is, without oppressing, humiliating, or crushing our spirits. All that I have wanted to do here is to raise some questions about the kinds of presuppositions you (and many others, of course) bring to the hearing of any Christian testimony to divine presence, transcendence, and mystery. Some of those presuppositions are themselves questionable, and they may be functioning in your life as false and unnecessary blocks to your hearing of that testimony. We seem to be living at a time when the world itself, through costly trial and error, has rediscovered its own spiritual needs—or started to. Your social environment is no longer *monolithically* secular, no longer by definition hostile to transcendence.

But now to this quite positive assessment of the new spirituality of our society, I have to add a caveat—a small note of warning. Christians have to be a little skeptical also about *this* trend. The line between "spirituality" and "spiritual*ism*" is a very fine one; and an ideology (an "ism") of the *spirit* is just as questionable as an ideology of matter or any other "ism."

Listen, in the name of spirituality, all kinds of monstrous things have occurred in history, ancient and modern. Nothing in the modern world has been so "spiritual" as the mass rallies of Hitler's Nazis at Nüremberg and elsewhere. Those meetings were full of ecstatic, wildly enthusiastic people, wholly "turned on" by a highly spiritualized worldview, one celebrating the exalted spirit of the Aryan race and its allegedly redemptive mission in the world.

We have seen tragic displays of "spirituality" in North America, too, with innocent and naive and tragically misled people giving themselves over to absurd theories and orgies of true belief and senseless self-sacrifice. Just because something announces itself as "spirituality" does not mean that Christians should rejoice in it! To the contrary, they should probably exercise greater critical vigilance in the presence of spiritualizers than in any other context. After all, biblically speaking, the *greatest* spirit of all—great in a way that deluded human beings always recognize greatness—is the one the Bible calls Satan, "the Father of Lies" (John 8:44), as distinct, remember, from the "truth" into which, Jesus says, the *divine* Spirit will lead his followers. Demonic spirits are *always* the more impressive ones—they are those who bring on the real fireworks! *God's* Spirit, on the contrary, is a "still small voice" (1 Kings 19:12), a quiet influence—perhaps no more impressive than the words of a simple person, even a child (Matt. 21:16), or the faces of the poor and sick and needy. *God's* Spirit, in the biblical understanding, does not come on strong. If we are in the end overpowered by it, it is only because we want to be—because we, like Jacob at the brook, while wrestling with that Spirit are really longing to be blessed by it (Gen. 32:22-32).

So, while the new spirituality can provide a necessary criticism of modernity's simplistic trust of technical rationality; while it can offer something like a new framework of credibility for Christian and other religious faith, it must not be seen as an obvious or unquestionably trustworthy friend of Christian belief. It remains true—what the same author of John's Gospel wrote in his first letter—that the spirits must be "tested" (1 John 4:1-6). Not all spirits are "of God," he says; in fact, he implies that most are not! So one must check them out. They will be known for what they are by the kinds of things that they entice their adherents to do, say, think, and believe. Spirits that manifest themselves in unusual displays of a suprahuman or seemingly godlike nature are held in high suspicion by the Bible. Jesus did not attempt to impress people and commend himself by resorting to such tactics; on the contrary, he resisted all such temptations as being "of the devil" (Matt. 4:1-11; Luke 4:1-12). And the life of Jesus, says John, is the "test" to which reputed spirits and their representatives have to be put. Some Christians will disagree with me here and point to the miracles of Jesus; but the miracles are really about something else—in fact, they are about that same "healing" and "wholeness" that we discussed last time: they are parables and exemplifications of salvation.

When it comes to spirits and spiritualism, what serious Christians should remember is not so much the miracles of Jesus as his many conversations with people, his way of being with them. He did not *command* belief in them; where possible, he *evoked* faith, but he did not cause them to believe because of fantastic displays of power. Jesus was willing to trust language; he did people the great honor of discoursing with them reasonably; he did not want to thrust change upon them, but to help it to happen within them—through the ordinary processes of thought, the deepening and renewing of the mind. Jesus did not violate their understanding, however limited and frustrating it might be, by overpowering it through mystic spiritual means—that would have been to turn the miraculous into pure magic. If their understanding were to be awakened to the truly transcendent and mysterious, if they were to know themselves—as the disciples came to know themselves—to be "standing under" something infinitely greater than they could ever understand, this would have to happen from within, not as something imposed from without.

And that is why Paul, who doesn't altogether rule out external signs of the Holy Spirit's presence such as *glossolalia* or "speaking in tongues," nevertheless warns his churches against such practices. He would rather, he writes, say "five words" that make sense than to babble on in some unheard of jibberish that might impress sensation-seeking or perhaps neurotic people, but would do nothing for genuine faith—unless it were then clearly interpreted (1 Cor. 14:18-19).

And so we are back at "reasons." As I said before, I doubt if faith ever comes to anyone as a result of argumentation, reasoning, proving this and that. It is indeed a gift of the Spirit if I believe, or, to speak more accurately, if my native *unbelief* is perennially challenged by its opposite. Faith is not just my doing—not just the conclusions of the mind. If it were simply a human possibility, I'd certainly try to argue you into it!—because I do think it would make all the difference for you.

I can't do that. But what I can do, or try to do, is to help you to look more closely at your own options as someone who lives in our kind of world. For a couple of centuries and more, ours has been a fact-befuddled world that advertises itself as "scientific" and "rational" and (of course!) "practical." Over against that "secular" worldview a new concern for "spirit" has arisen, and faith can relate positively to that concern at many points. But Christian faith is not an "ism"—it is no more a spiritualism than it is a materialism. Faith keeps its own counsel, follows its own drumbeat. If against secularism and rationalism it calls for more spirit, against spiritualism it calls for greater faithfulness to this world and to the ordinary processes of human thinking. The pendulum of human historical preferences is always swinging. It goes from one extreme to another, and in the process lives are affected—many, alas, are literally lost, for ideologies are never harmless! Christianity is not just a matter of keeping one's balance in the midst of all this—no, it is not just a matter of balance and "the middle way." But there is, I think, a kind of sanity about it, when it is well understood, which in the name of the "abundant life" that is the goal of its Lord and Spirit, resists all those "isms" that promise great things but in the end, and with great regularity, rob humanity of its birthright.

What's the Difference?

five

It had been "one of those days." Too many meetings, too many phone calls, too much busy work. Besides, I hadn't slept well the night before. I even forgot that we'd arranged to meet that day at four, so I'm afraid I wasn't very welcoming when you appeared at my door. Fortunately, you didn't seem to notice that. You had your own agenda, and (such is the power of ideas) you soon enticed me into it—and in the process redeemed a day that I'd more or less given up on.

"Your last piece ended in a way that surprised me," you began. "I mean that part about Christianity being 'sane.'"

"Why did that surprise you?" I asked.

You hesitated. Then: "I'm not quite sure. I think it had something to do with trying to put such an idea together with the Christians I actually know, or hear about. On the one hand, there are the good, middle-class types who go to the 'nice' churches—the pretty churches where their sons and daughters can have pretty weddings, you know. I know quite a few of those people. Some of them are my close relatives. They're certainly 'sane,' if by that you mean well-balanced, well-adjusted, predictable, respectable. They don't go in for wildness or exaggeration in any form—not publicly, at any rate. They don't talk in loud voices, usually. They're . . . reasonable. If that's what 'sane' means—well, I suppose there are worse things, but it's sure not very exciting!"

"And on the other hand. . . ?" I put in.

"On the other hand there are the really earnest *types—some of them to the point of being fanatics," you answered. "I don't know many of them personally, but who can live here without knowing about them? I'm talking about the people who 'get converted,' are 'true believers,' go on the offensive. Some talk in tongues, others stand on street corners with signs about the end of the world, have visions, and so on. Typically, their preachers get all worked up—they don't talk, they yell. And the congregations don't sit there quietly, as happens in the 'nice' churches, with people smiling sweetly and listening politely to some 'meaningful' sermon. No, they all become really involved. They shout out 'Amens' and 'Hallelujahs.' Sometimes there's drama—somebody falls down in a fit of Spirit-possession. And so on.*

"Now that," you went on, "is definitely not *sane—not by our usual standards, anyway. But it certainly considers itself* Christian. *And, in fact, it seems to me, that kind of Christianity is on the increase in North America, while the respectable, sober kind is declining—maybe because, in the end, you can't tell it from the wallpaper; I mean, it's so 'sane' that it seems indistinguishable from everything else the middle class goes in for. Disneyland with religion."*

"So what are you asking?" I wanted to know.

"I think what I'd really like to talk about is what Christianity 'is,' or 'does'—that is, what difference does it make? What would it mean to live in a 'Christian' way? How does Christianity change people? See what I mean?"

I waited for you to go on. I knew what you were getting at, of course, but I wanted to hear more.

"You said that Christianity has some kind of sanity about it," you continued after a little. "I think I like that idea. I think so. But I'm still unclear about what it means to you. If it means the sort of thing I associate with the churches I've gone to on various occasions—I think they're called 'mainstream' or something—then it doesn't seem to involve anything different from . . . you know . . . 'business as usual.' So why bother? On the other hand, the people who take their

Christianity most seriously in this country don't strike me as being what most people I know would call 'sane.' Christian faith obviously does make a real difference to fundamentalists and evangelicals and other such enthusiasts. But it's not the kind of difference I find at all attractive, frankly.

"So I guess what I am asking is, Should Christianity make a difference? And if so, what would the difference look like? . . . Is there a risk that if someone like me decided to become a Christian I'd be changed into another kind of person altogether?—maybe one of the yelling preachers or something?"

"Who knows what you might become?" I remarked. "That would depend on a great many things—such as the kind of Christianity that got through to you, and whether it was followed up with any sort of serious study of the Bible and other Christian literature, and what sort of Christian community you were associated with—among other things."

"I guess I know that," you said. "But let's assume that 'the kind of Christianity that got through to me' was your kind, and that you would then help to guide my study, and that you would also help me to find a Christian community, a church: What difference would it make? How would I be changed? Or would I?"

This was becoming a little uncomfortable for both of us, wasn't it? Did I detect more than an "academic" interest in the subject on your part? And how, if that were the case, could I make the switch from "professor" to "confessor"? How do that without imposing upon you, trespassing on your privacy?

"I don't know how you'd be changed," I answered after a rather awkward pause. "I can't predict such things—and I don't even want to. That's something between yourself and . . ." (I nearly said "and your conscience," but then I remembered something; I'll tell you about that later) "—between yourself and God."

Was I hedging? Did I just want to avoid that kind of personal encounter? Probably. Partly. It's hard for someone like me, conditioned as I am by decades of "professional" Christianity, to take on the role of witness to the faith. Besides, did I have the right to assume that role with you? It's so easy to become manipulative. Being the teacher gives one an unfair advantage sometimes. I knew you liked me, trusted me—even thought of me as a friend. After all those hours of conversation over the past weeks, you would probably take what I said quite seriously—perhaps too seriously. And then there was the more subtle temptation: that with a certain part of yourself you would like me to make this kind of a leap for you.

In any case, rightly or wrongly, I chose to keep our conversation a little more objective—not impersonal, I think, but . . . general.

"*There is no one way in which to live as a Christian,*" *I told you.* "*No standard pattern. And that's as it should be. Because you are not a human clone, or a 'type,' or a 'case.' You are who you are. And, according to my understanding of this faith, it is the aim of the gospel to help you to become who you are—who you are essentially; not to impose upon you some completely new sort of personhood, but to give you the courage, imagination, and will that you need in order to grow into the really human person that is already there in you, potentially, waiting to be born.*

"*A lot of 'stuff' gets in the way of your being that person, as you yourself know better than I do. There are certain fears, certain anxieties, certain pretensions and influences that keep you from becoming who you really are. Do you know what I mean? For instance, you want to make an impression on someone—perhaps even sometimes on me! So you put on a certain front, you emphasize some aspects of your character and hide others, you playact a little. And in the process you deceive both the other person and yourself—except that you know, underneath it all, that you have done this.*

"*Or to take a different kind of example, let's say that you are really afraid of something—that your chances of a successful future are jeopardized by the increasing takeover of human occupations by computers. But instead of talking about this openly you conceal it, and when you're with your friends you try to create the impression that you're really up-to-date, computer-literate, and terribly keen about all the wonderful things cybernetics are going to make possible. So, over the years, you develop a kind of public persona that is at odds* with your private thoughts. In other words, you squelch within yourself the kind of honesty that might in fact be rather beneficial, not only to yourself but to your society. You become a conformist.[1]

"I believe that the function of faith in one's life, understood in a Christian way at least, is to clear away all the debris that gets in the way of our being who we are—or who we could become, and to help us to become mature, full grown, fully human. So of course this has to differ from person to person, because no one of us is quite the same as anyone else."

"You mean that Christianity is individualistic?" you asked.

"No, definitely not individualistic!" I replied. "But it is concerned about the individual, the self. And its great interest in creating community, in bringing people and indeed all creatures into harmony with one another, should never be interpreted to mean that the individual human being is unimportant or merely secondary. Jesus carried on some very significant public discourses, according to the Gospels; but a great deal of what is recorded of him there has to do with his encounters with individual persons, and he never has quite the same thing to say to each one—for the obvious reason that each one is a unique human being and needs a specific sort of 'salvation' if he or she is to become 'whole.' (Remember what we were saying about salvation?).

"In that connection, there's a very interesting little scene described at the end of John's Gospel [21:20-23]. The risen Jesus has been telling Peter what he expects of him in future, and suddenly Peter points to the disciple John, of whom he is perhaps a little jealous, and asks, 'Lord, what about him?' And Jesus replies: 'If it is my will that he remain until I come, what is that to you? Follow me!' In other words, 'Your story is your story, and his story is his.'

"You asked what difference is made by Christian faith, and finally, I think, the answer has to be something like that: It depends upon who you are, what you are called to be and become. Here the 'story' is always uniquely one's own. So I cannot answer your question very well, certainly not in a specific way. Your life, if you become a Christian, will be the answer.

"But what I can do, perhaps—and it's what I plan to try doing after I've had time to think about this conversation—is to respond to your question in a more general sort of way: What is the kind of difference that Christian faith makes in people's lives? Perhaps on the basis of such an overview, so to speak, you will be able to make some applications to your own 'story.'"

Faith, Hope, and Love

When I considered our last talk, and how best to describe what difference Christian belief makes in people's lives, it seemed to me that there would be no better way of doing that than by reflecting on the three qualities that Paul names in one of the best-known passages of his writings (the thirteenth chapter of his first letter to the little church he had started at Corinth): faith, hope, and love. They've been called the three "Christian virtues," though I'm personally somewhat uncomfortable with that way of speaking about them. The passage is devoted mainly to Paul's description of love—and it's a remarkably beautiful bit of writing, especially when you consider that it was done by a confirmed old bachelor!

> If I speak in the tongues of mortals and of angels, but do not have love, I am a noisy gong or a clanging cymbal. And if I have prophetic powers, and understand all mysteries and all knowledge, and if I have all faith, so as to remove mountains, but do not have love, I am nothing. If I give away all my possessions, and if I hand over my body so that I may boast, but do not have love, I gain nothing.
>
> Love is patient; love is kind; love is not envious or boastful or arrogant or rude. It does not insist on its own way; it is not irritable or resentful; it does not rejoice in wrongdoing, but rejoices in the truth. It bears all things, believes all things, hopes all things, endures all things.
>
> Love never ends. But as for prophecies, they will come to an end; as for tongues, they will cease; as for knowledge, it will come

to an end. For we know only in part, and we prophesy only in part; but when the complete comes, the partial will come to an end. When I was a child, I spoke like a child, I thought like a child, I reasoned like a child; when I became an adult, I put an end to childish ways. For now we see in a mirror, dimly, but then we will see face to face. Now I know only in part; then I will know fully, even as I have been fully known. And now faith, hope, and love abide, these three; and the greatest of these is love.

While Paul concentrates here on love, he brings to that discussion a profound and long-considered understanding of both of the other qualities that "abide," faith and hope. And if in the long run he is compelled to say that, of the three, love is "the greatest," this is not intended to minimize the significance of faith and hope. On the contrary, faith and hope are for him the *presuppositions* of love; because he is not just talking about human love, but of the love of God—a love that we come to know *through* faith and hope in God. So before we think about "the greatest" difference that Christian belief can make in people, we'll consider what we may think of as the differences that make *that* difference possible.

Faith

First, *faith*. What does this little word mean? You may recall that we thought about it, briefly, in our first meeting—that conversation that prompted me to describe how, over against the moralism of my village church, I found myself strangely attracted to what Paul said about being "justified by grace through faith, not by works . . ." and so on. But now we have to ask, what *is* faith?

There are so many *bad* preconceptions of faith at work in our society, not least of all in the churches, that in order to define it as positively as I can I'll have first to say what I think it is *not*. (Do you remember that we used this approach, the "way of negation," when we thought about God?)

First: <u>Faith is *not* to be thought of as giving one's assent</u> to a number of propositions or ideas or doctrines—such as, "God is one substance in three persons," "God forgives sins because of the perfect sacrifice of Jesus," "The Bible is God's own Word," and so on. Faith certainly *involves* doctrines. I mean, it presupposes one's having lived with and thought about a whole cluster of claims and ideas—ideas about God, about the Christ, about creation, and so forth; but it *is* not these ideas or our acceptance of such. If I equate faith with giving credence to Christian theological ideas about God, it is rather like equating my trust in my wife with certain conceptions that I have of her, certain conclusions *I've* drawn about her over the years. My faith in my wife is not my decision to trust my own ideas of her, but to trust *her*—a person, a "thou," whom I can never capture or contain in ideas and propositions, even good ones. In relation to the person my wife actually *is*, my ideas about her are strictly relative even when they are fairly accurate. Faith in God is similar to that.

Second: <u>Faith is *not* certainty, or certitude.</u> Paul makes a distinction between "faith" and "sight." Just now, under the conditions of historical existence, we do not and cannot "know for certain"; we cannot "see," or as he says, we see only "as in a mirror, dimly." He believes in a future when we *shall* see and understand fully what now we can only vaguely anticipate; but for the present our condition is that of being on the way to that future, not of having arrived. "On the way" to any destination, the appropriate attitude is to trust, so far as one can, whoever is (so to speak) "in the driver's seat," not to behave as though one were personally in charge, or had already reached the end of the journey.

Third: <u>Faith is *not* just a sort of "believing" attitude, a pleasant and positive human virtue.</u> That's one reason I don't much like speaking of these "qualities" as "virtues," because none of them—neither faith, nor hope, nor love—is something a person can conjure up and work on, as one might work, for example, on being kind and considerate. Many people in the more liberal and moderate churches—the "nice" churches, as you called them—when they think of "faith" think of it this way: it's a "nice" way to be; people without it tend not to be "nice." It's as if faith were a quality of one's personality, something one could cultivate, like hospitality or charm or friendliness or good manners. I suppose I know what people mean when they talk this way, but it's not what the Bible means by faith. It may be a by-product of faith in some way, but it is not the thing itself.

Now, in describing what I think faith *isn't*, I've already implied something of what I believe it *is*. Let me try now to state a positive definition more explicitly. I'll make three observations, each one in turn correlated with the negative points I have already made:

First: I would say that faith is something that occurs within a relationship—it is one's response to God. Relationship with God has to be presupposed, and that is true of all three of these "abiding" qualities: they all presuppose God's presence as One who has become "real" for one. God has made Godself known to one in somewhat the way we've already discussed this—in the particularity of Jesus, through the testimony of the divine Spirit. One feels God is "there" for one, is "with" one; and one responds to this Presence with trust—in some such way as I respond to the presence of my spouse, or of a friend who has demonstrated his or her trustworthiness, with trust from my side. Faith is our response to God's faithfulness.

This is why faith can't be thought of as mere *intellectual* assent to ideas about God and so on. Faith is a category of *relationship*—something that happens, not in my isolation as one who is perhaps "thinking about" God, or reckoning on the possibility of God's existence, or speculating about the divine in an abstract way; rather, faith occurs in relation to the experienced presence of God. So it is faith *in*, not faith *that*. This is why the most important historic creeds of the church[2] begin, "I believe *in* God . . ." not "I believe *that* God is omnipotent, etc., etc."

Second: faith is *trust*, we said, and not certainty; and therefore it implies certain possibilities that tend to disappear if faith is turned into religious certitude (that is, what some people call "true belief.") It is particularly important to realize, I think, that faith understood as trust respects the integrity and freedom of the person: it assumes personal decision, just as all profound human relationships do. The presence of God, as we said in connection with the work of the Holy Spirit, does not impose itself on a person so that he or she has no choice in the matter. Yes, as with intense forms of human love for instance, there is a dimension of being "overwhelmed" by God's love; but what this love of God wants, after all, is our trust, *our* love in return; and not even God can have such reciprocity by *forcing* us to love and trust. Love can't be compelled. If it is, it isn't love any longer. So faith as trust in God's gracious love for us, however much it may be drawn or evoked by the quality and extent of God's love, maintains our freedom to love.

By the same token, it also maintains—and this is just as important!—our freedom to hold back and to *doubt*. Trust implies decision, and decision implies considering both the yes and the no: to trust or not to trust? In all of our human relationships, if they are real, we are always making that decision. When we stop deciding, the relationship has probably come to an end. Someone who really loves me gives me the freedom to make up my mind—not just once, but time and again, and, really, all the time. Life, the real *life* that is in the relationship, depends on this—even though the relationship is never *entirely* secure on that account. But then, so-called "secure" relationships are usually not relationships at all, but perhaps has-been-relationships: relationships of the past into which far too much presumption and taking-for-granted has crept.

Similarly, faith in God requires continuous decision—not always the *agonizing* decision that is associated with initial decision making, but nevertheless decision. And what this means is that doubt is permitted, too. In fact, it's assumed. "Faith that does not doubt is dead faith" (Miguel de Unamuno). It doesn't make sense to say that you "trust" if you have no personal acquaintance with distrust. So, far from being something forbidden to "the faithful Christian," doubt is part of the Christian life. In a real way, one could say, God expects us to doubt; because without doubt our belief in God becomes just as routine and artificial as happens in human relationships that have lost their vitality. So don't let anyone tell you that if you have any doubt in you, you don't believe in God, or that Christian faith has no room for unfaith. The most poignant—and accurate—prayer of the Christian is always rather like the statement of a man to Jesus in the newer Testament: "Lord, I believe, help my unbelief" (Mark 9:24).

Besides, there is another kind of logic in this believing/doubting life of the Christian and the Christian community—and we should remember this when we speak, as I hope we will later, about "the church." What I'm referring to is this: Without the doubting side of faith, how could the Christian church ever relate to the *world* of doubt and disbelief? As it is, unfortunately, one of the greatest reasons that our world has so much trouble believing Christians is that the Christians so characteristically exaggerate their belief and hide their doubt! If Christians were a little more open and honest about their *questions*, I think, their *answers* might be more intriguing to those outside the churches.

Third: When Christians speak of faith they mean something real, something vital, and therefore not (as I said earlier) something that can be cultivated, imitated, manufactured, worked on. Faith occurs in relationship, it is not a matter of self-help. What governs faith is the relationship with God that has brought it about and sustains it. So faith is not to be equated with qualities like "positive thinking" and "cheerfulness" and "joy" and "celebration" and so forth. Of course some of those qualities may be consequences of faith—one hopes that they will be—and usually they are, though by no means exclusively. For faith should also be associated with qualities that many "nice" people don't want to cultivate—like critical awareness, judicious thought, the capacity to make distinctions, sorrow, suffering, lamentation, even anger. Yes, genuinely faithful Christians will often be sorrowful or angry; because they will see in the world and in their own lives things that the love of God does not desire and cannot condone. When faith is too restrictively associated with what we generally assume to be desirable, "positive" virtues, most of the *prophetic* side of faith biblically understood is just ruled out in advance. By "prophetic" I mean the courage to see and to name what is wrong with the world, to the end that it might be changed, righted. And that may be why the "nice" churches, as you call them, have so little to do with the big, scary social issues of our times. For none of those issues can be contemplated or confronted in exclusively "positive" ways.

What I've said here certainly doesn't exhaust the meaning of faith, but maybe it's enough to give you some idea of the general direction of my thought on this matter. At least it may be sufficient to let me address your big question: What difference might faith, understood in these ways, make? We could reflect on such a question endlessly, of course. The "difference" made by faith will differ from person to person, since what faith changes will depend on what is there to be changed. My own answer to the question will inevitably be colored by my particular experience, and since I have no wish to conceal that from you I'll illustrate through personal reference something of what difference I think faith makes.

First: One of the most important differences faith makes, in my experience, is that it makes possible a greater—well, let me put it this way, a greater *nonchalance* about oneself. By that I certainly don't mean recklessness or apathy or being "cool"; but faith in God relieves one, I think, of the burden of excessive self-concern.

To illustrate: I am by nature something of a worrier. I think I always have been—and who knows why? Is it the result of being the eldest child in a large family? Or is it perhaps because I grew up during the great Depression? Or was it the sheer secularism of the age into which I was born? Probably all of these factors contributed, and more. I do think that the general agnosticism of our society has bred a lot of fretfulness that is seldom understood as a by-product of secularity. The secular mind thinks, "I am myself responsible for everything. 'There ain't no George.'" At its best, this sense of responsibility has achieved some very admirable things throughout our modern epoch. Because we didn't wait for "George" (God, Fate, History) to do away with debilitating diseases like polio or tuberculosis, but tried to assume real responsibility for their cure, we live now in a world that is not so gravely threatened in those particular ways.

But by the same token, the secular mentality creates in people—and I mean in good, admirable, conscientious people—an enormous burden: We feel we are responsible for "everything," but we know that we can't manage "everything." In the public sphere as in our personal lives, we are often overwhelmed by the impossibility of our lot. "What can anyone *do*?" we ask one another again and again. I doubt if it would be possible to overestimate the tremendous burden felt today by persons in public office, when they are conscientious and sincere. So many perils to be averted, so many different historical exigencies to be planned for, and so far in advance, and so many forces at work against concerted and well-meaning human efforts to ensure the triumph of the good! In private life, especially in societies (including ours) that are becoming less and less oriented toward public welfare, more and more individualistic—in these societies the economic, vocational, and psychological responsibility of the individual person and the family increases daily. As a habitual worrier, I know that I am not alone today. Certainly human beings have always worried—why wouldn't they? But it's one thing to worry when you are up against forces you know are not controllable anyway, and another when you feel you should have control, could have prevented this and that, are responsible for everything.

Faith, I would say, puts all this into perspective. Of course it must do so again and again, not only once; but it does do that—if I can rely on my own experience. For faith in God is faith *in God*. I mean, it is trust in One who is *ultimately* responsible, and who as such is *trustworthy*. Trusting God, one can go about one's tasks in life with greater confidence. At least one can begin to do that, to be a little more relaxed. It is no longer necessary to behave as if everything were against you, as if you had to keep second-guessing where the next blow would come from in order to fend it off in advance! Life, History, the World: these are not impersonal, random things that play with one's existence as a cat plays with a wounded sparrow. Even sparrows matter to God, Jesus said; even the hairs of our heads are numbered (Matt. 6:25ff.). In other words, the relationship of faith in God creates in us the kind of trust that spills over into all aspects of life. It enables us to put our worry and carefulness in its place—which is *not* at the forefront of our thinking!—and to trust that, appearances notwithstanding, life itself is "on our side." Not for merely sentimental, humanistic reasons, but because the God we trust is the Lord of life and only wishes, as we saw earlier, that we should have life more abundantly. Second, there is closely connected dimension of faith that I must immediately introduce in order to prevent the first point from being misunderstood: trusting God does *not* mean, in my opinion, that one can simply lie back and "let God [alias George] do it." I said that faith helps one to achieve a certain nonchalance about one's life—not that it is presumptuous. We human beings cannot do everything—we simply cannot! And it is vain and absurd for us to think we can. But there are some things that we can do, and indeed that *only* we can do; and so if faith means being freed *from* the burden and the worry that goes with imagining ourselves "gods," it also means being freed *for* the responsibility that goes with our being men and women.

This is why faith, as it is used in the Bible, so frequently goes together with "calling" or vocation. Jesus not only asks people to trust him, but to follow him—to become disciples. As *followers* they know they are not "in charge"; they are not expected to "do it all." But they are expected to follow, and that involves discipline, rigor, sacrifice, suffering. They are not going to change the world all by themselves—because they are not all by themselves! They are "not alone."[3] But they have their specific callings, each one unique, and, individually, they contribute to the work of the whole body.

So while the Bible, unlike modernity, does not elevate the human species to the position of mastery in the world, it does have a "high" conception of the place of Homo sapiens in the scheme of things: we are stewards of the mysteries and the mercies of God, says Paul (1 Cor. 4:1), summing up the responsibility that belongs to Christ's followers and, in doing so, speaking about human vocation generally. We are stewards. Not owners, and not mere slaves either; but responsible servants, with a mandate to serve and the talents necessary to fulfill it.[4]

Third: Another major difference that faith makes, in my experience, is that it supports that within each one of us that wants to be truthful—that wants to know the truth, and to experience the kind of freedom that only truth can give one. "If you continue in my word, you are truly my disciples," said Jesus, "and you will know the truth, and the truth will make you free" (John 8:31-32). It seems to me that this longing for truth really does exist in the human mind and heart. But most of us, most of the time, are afraid to pursue that longing too far. As psychologists have told us, we "repress" a great deal of the truth—truth about ourselves, about our relatives and friends, about our world as a whole—because we feel intuitively that we just couldn't handle it. And the fact is, we probably couldn't; so in that sense "repressing" it—pushing it under the carpet before it becomes visible!—is often a good, or at least a necessary, thing.

But it can also be a bad and dangerous thing. Individuals can become so "repressive" in relation to the truth about their condition that they cause all the other people who must live near them to suffer. The others are blamed for the problems that one cannot deal with oneself. And we could even talk about this on the level of society, because there are whole societies that are so fearful of truth, of reality, that they blame other societies for their own recurring problems. In America, for instance, a good deal of the anticommunism that surfaced during the Cold War period has to be explained by that kind of public repression.

Human beings, both socially and individually, try to keep going by emphasizing what they consider their positive assets and concealing their liabilities. The trouble is, unrecognized or concealed liabilities are the most dangerous ones. They eat away at life silently, like the microscopic creatures that cause malaria. An individual consistently incapable of facing the truth about his violence toward his wife and children may well become still more violent on account of his refusal to admit and to reflect upon his behavior. A society that believes itself terribly advanced and refuses, perhaps for that reason, to consider the millions of poor people within its own borders, may in the end be destroyed by its failure to pursue truth as vigorously as it pursues "success" and "happiness."

In other words, truth—and particularly truth concerning what is wrong with us, or with our world—is probably the most important requirement for survival; certainly it's one of the most important ingredients for that integrity and wholeness (*salus*) that we already discussed. Without an orientation toward truth there will be neither compassion nor justice.

But to pursue truth as vigorously and intelligently as one can, one needs to have a great deal of support—the kind of support that assures one, in effect, that even though exposure to the truth may turn out to be terribly painful, it will be possible to bear it. The needed undergirding will be there.

Faith, when it is genuine, is just such undergirding. Trusting in God, I discover what I know I have little of within myself: the courage to be truthful. And I don't say this just in a pious way; there is a very good "reason" for saying it. Because what it means is that the one who trusts God knows that the truth she or he must face is always only just part—perhaps just a very small part—of a much greater truth, God's truth. And God's truth, which faith only grasps in a beginning sort of way, is so expansive and so orientated toward *love*, as Paul says in the Corinthians quotation, that it is able to absorb and overcome even the most frightening truths that human beings must encounter in their sojourn through time.

I have always appreciated in that connection a verse from the first epistle of John: ". . . by this we will know that we are from the truth and will reassure our hearts before [God] whenever our hearts condemn us; for God is greater than our hearts, and he knows everything" (1 John 3:19-20). Many people place a lot of emphasis on "conscience," and probably that isn't such a bad thing; but the conscience can also be a biased arbiter, and not infrequently a real tyrant. Well, here is a biblical writer who says that the conscience (in Hebraic thought called "the heart"), while it is undoubtedly important, is not the most important judge of what is ultimately the case: God is much greater. Our consciences always do know something against us, and nine times out of ten they will use that knowledge to condemn us—which is why, I suppose, modern people have been so glad to find out from the psychologists that the conscience is just something implanted in us by our parents and mentors and society! All the same, we don't like to be reminded by our conscience of all the "negative data" they hang on to. That's what we habitually repress. But faith believes in One who "knows everything," not only what is to be said against us. And that One, as John puts it so simply and directly in this same letter, "is love." So in the presence of the loving, *all*-knowing God, faith receives the courage to open itself to the truth that is usually hidden—truth that can only be faced when one has the assurance that it is not *all* the truth.

Fourth: There is one more thing that I feel I should say about faith—one, among the many things I'll have to leave unsaid just now—and it is that faith has a way of pushing one into a deeper and deeper search for those "reasons" that we have been looking for throughout these discussions. Faith is not just a "blind" affair, as it is sometimes thought. It doesn't say, "I'll believe it no matter what it is. I accept everything!" No, faith, if it is authentic, gives birth to a thirst for knowledge—even for wisdom. If someone like you, for instance, got to the place in your contemplation where you were able to say, "Yes, I think this is for me," well, that initial "leap of faith," as Søren Kierkegaard called it, would only be the beginning. If it were real faith, and not just sentimentality or a holy glow, it would—if I may put it this way—take you by the lapels and say, "Now, friend, let's get down to business."

And this "down to business" would mean many things, but two in particular: first, it would mean immersing you in the world of human need. Remember what Jesus said to the young man we mentioned way back at the beginning: "Sell what you have, give to the poor, and come, follow me" (Matt. 19:21). That is, faith would require of you the kind of serious obedience that would involve a new and lasting concern for your own kind, and for otherkind—indeed, today we must say for the world as a whole. That would be part of the "calling," the "vocation" that faith in God entails.

But, second, "getting down to business" would mean becoming serious as a thinker and student of "the faith." When you asked me what would happen to you if you became a Christian, I replied that among other things that would depend upon whether you were then introduced to any disciplined sort of study of Christianity, the Scriptures, and the great literature of the faith. Certainly if you became the sort of Christian I would like to see you become one day, it would not be only as an activist or only as a pious person—though I have no wish to belittle either activity or piety, far from it! But today in particular the kinds of Christians the world needs are persons who have committed themselves to some depths of *understanding*. They would not use their study of the Scriptures and traditions of the faith to excuse them either from worldly responsibility or prayer, but they would also not be satisfied with a Christian faith that was active and prayerful yet, at the level of understanding, remained at the kindergarten stage.

And all I am doing here is accentuating what one of the great seers of the Christian movement said long ago—Anselm, who became Bishop of Canterbury in the eleventh century: "Faith seeks understanding," he wrote, meaning, "If it's the real thing, it will not be satisfied with 'causes,' it will want to continue all through life to explore the 'reasons' for what it believes." Today this has to be emphasized more than ever before, because there is a lot of Christianity in the world—and especially in North America, I would say—that is *unreasoning* and *unreasonable*. And this is not a harmless thing, a minor fault; it is the source of foolish and dangerous beliefs and lifestyles—beliefs and lifestyles that, among other things, keep many people like you from considering Christianity a live option for your own lives. Real faith doesn't demand of human beings that they turn off their brains; on the contrary, faith *activates* our minds, liberating us from intellectual sloth and caution, freeing us from ancient taboos and superstitions, and implanting in us a new curiosity about everything under the sun. That, too, belongs to the "abundant life" that God wills for us.

Hope

We thought a little, earlier, about the second of Paul's "abiding" qualities, *hope*, but now we're considering it from another perspective—the difference that it makes in the lives of Christians.

First, however, we'll have to establish what we mean by hope. Hope is a word that flows easily from the lips of North Americans. We like to consider ourselves a "hopeful" sort of people, and so the rhetoric of our public figures—especially at times of elections— must be laced with optimism. But Christian hope is not a synonym for optimism.

I have nothing against optimism, when it's the real thing. When one meets a genuinely optimistic person it's usually a very pleasant experience. On the other hand, nothing is more unconvincing and deceptive than the sort of optimism that is the result of someone's sheer determination to "think positively." And in my experience a good deal of what calls itself optimism today, in both the private and the public sectors, is of the latter variety!

If you think carefully about what's wrong with such "determined" optimism, you'll begin to appreciate the difference between optimism and hope. People who grit their teeth and insist on being optimistic are obviously trying to forget about something, overlook something, erase something from their thoughts. They don't want to dwell on all the things in their lives that make them feel despondent or afraid or melancholy. They think they can rid themselves of all that "negativity" if only they concentrate hard enough on what they consider positive. In other words, we're back at "repression": this kind of fabricated optimism is a clumsy way of repressing everything that might make one *pessimistic*.

There are, of course, times when a person must do just that— be deliberately "positive." One can admire such determination as a temporary measure, a way of "carrying on." But as a habitual way of coping, a way of life, it is not only ineffective but, often enough, it results in even greater problems than those that it was supposed to solve. Reality will out, and when it is not allowed to come out openly and consciously it will find other exits that are in the end usually more painful.

To illustrate: I once knew a man whose greatest energies were spent on pathetic attempts to make the externalities of his life (his own person and attire, his house, his car, his wife, his children— and approximately in that order!) conform to the high ideal of successful living that he had entertained, I suppose, from his childhood onward. But what was most evident about his situation (one felt it in his presence always) was a terrible frustration, amounting sometimes almost to frenzy. The cause of this was obvious to all his friends: reality would simply not conform to his great expectations. His clothes were never fashionable enough, his house was never big enough, his car was never powerful or new enough, his children were never successful enough, and his wife (for reasons obvious enough to the onlooker) had periods of very bad humor. The point is, however, that the greatest single reason for the unhappiness of the whole family was the man's refusal to allow any unhappiness. His determination to consider only what he called "the brighter side" had become a kind of tyranny affecting everyone in his immediate circle.

Human beings must hope. Without hope life itself cannot be sustained for very long, and civilization is impossible. It was no accident that when Dante in his *Inferno* wanted his readers to understand the depths of evil, he pictured the gates of hell with these words written over them: "Abandon hope, all ye who enter here." So it is completely understandable and human when people work terribly hard at hoping, as did the man of my illustration. It is part of the real pathos of life that we are so often driven to such lengths in our attempts to acquire this precious quality. We seem to know intuitively that without hope life itself will wither and die. One felt sorry for this man, because he was attempting so desperately to get a stranglehold on hope.

For Christians, however, hope is precisely not something that you can "get"—that you can manufacture out of the raw stuff of life and through your own sheer determination. For Christians, rather, hope is a gift. It is given together with faith, and is nothing more nor less than one of faith's many dimensions. It is faith applied to the future. As I reminded you, faith just means "trust." If one trusts God, one trusts God's ability and readiness to care for one in the future as in the present and past. To say the same thing in a slightly different way, one trusts the future to *God*—not to oneself, not to humankind as a whole, not to government, not to the church, not to history, not to some theory of progress, but to God. And therefore one is not thrown into disillusionment and confusion whenever the realities of one's life seem to lack any convincing evidence of hopefulness. For God's care of us and of the world—God's *providence*, as it is called traditionally—is often far from obvious to us. It is (again) a matter of faith, not of sight or certitude.

If we follow this theme of hope in the literature of the Bible, what strikes us again and again is the way that the people whose hope is "in God" are able to be completely honest about all the apparently hopeless things that happen to them. I don't mean that they welcome those things—far from it! There's no "death wish" in this story! But when these "bad things" happen to these (relatively!) "good people" they are kept going by their trust in God. Let's not exaggerate that trust. For most of us, it is only the beginnings of trust. But a little trust goes a long way. It enables one to believe that God is able to take all of the bad things into God's own Person and, in ways that we cannot predict, make them serve God's purposes. Even death, biblically understood, though it is "the last enemy" (1 Cor. 15:26), can in the long run only serve God's commitment to life, the life of the creation.

This theme is very prominent in the Jewish and Christian Scriptures. The older Testament's book of Job, which I urge you to read, is all about hope in dialogue with its opposite, despair. Job didn't deserve all the suffering that came his way, and he certainly didn't face it in a merely stoical way. It is misleading when people speak about "the patience of Job," because he wasn't all that patient; in fact, he became very angry, almost bitter; he came close to cursing God, as his loyal wife felt he would be justified in doing. But he never quite abandoned hope, because his hope was not in his riches or his achievements or even his family, but in God; and he believed that God could bring good out of evil, life out of death.

Or we could think of the intriguing story of Joseph and his brothers. It is not the usual sort of success story. Nothing protects Joseph from being badly hurt, physically and psychologically. If at nearly any point in his life he had tried to look on "the bright side" he would have found precious little evidence of it. Sold into slavery by his jealous brothers, he is subjected to one humiliation after another; and even at the end, after serving Egypt so faithfully, he has soon been forgotten by those in power. Eventually, Joseph understands—a little—why he had to go through all that misery. It was not just absurd, meaningless suffering after all. God wanted to preserve life at a time of famine and starvation. So (as Joseph says to his frightened brothers, finally), while they meant to do him harm, God, through their evil act, was able to achieve great good (Genesis 45).

And of course this same juxtaposition of despair and hope, suffering and salvation, is what informs the story that is for

Christians the very basis of their faith: Jesus, "crucified, dead and buried. . . ." There isn't much in the actual course of Jesus' life for the positive outlook to go on! As you rather crassly put it in one of our earlier discussions, from the perspective of the kind of success stories we like, Jesus was a failure—"dead at thirty-something" is how you phrased it, I remember. But if you study the Gospels carefully you'll notice that their authors have no intention of leaving out or minimizing the hopeless parts—including, as we have seen, the apparent hopelessness of Jesus himself, crying in abandonment from the cross (Matt. 27:46).

Of course, shallow religion wants us to think of the resurrection as if it simply cancelled out all that pain—as if now, after Easter, everything had been set to rights. But the resurrection doesn't cancel out the cross, it does something much better than that: It reveals the truth that God is present in the cross—in Jesus' cross, and therefore in all our crosses, whatever they may be. Hope therefore, resurrection hope, is not just Easter Sunday-optimism and lilies and "feeling good"; it is hope in the midst of the pain and despair into which life often leads us. It is what keeps us from capitulating to despair, while at the same time focused on life as it actually is, with its "darker" as well as its "brighter" sides.

Difference of Hope

So . . . what difference does such hope make? To me, it makes all the difference in the world. Again, I don't want to exaggerate—and, particularly, I don't want to overdo the extent of my own hopefulness. The truth is, I am not by nature a very hopeful person—yes, I admit it. I've already had to confess that I am a worrier, and obviously enough worriers worry in large measure because they are anxious about the future. The future, as someone said, always seems to be gathering itself for the attack!

The only kind of hope that I can entertain, therefore, is a hope that is able to do two things for me (if I may put it so baldly as that!): it must allow me to be as truthful as possible about the "bad things" that can and really do happen; and it must help me believe that those same "bad things" are not just meaningless but may be (*may* be!) the bearers of ultimate good. Or, to put it in another way, such hope must free me sufficiently from my anxious concern about tomorrow to enable me to enter more fully into life today. And that, I think, is what Jesus was getting at when he taught his followers—

> "Therefore I tell you, do not worry about your life, what you will eat or what you will drink, or about your body, what you will wear. Is not life more than food, and the body more than clothing? Look at the birds of the air; they neither sow nor reap nor gather into barns, and yet your heavenly Father feeds them. Are you not of more value than they? And can any of you by worrying add a single hour to your span of life? And why do you worry about clothing? Consider the lilies of the field, how they grow; they neither toil nor spin, yet I tell you, even Solomon in all his glory was not clothed like one of these. But if God so clothes the grass of the field, which is alive today and tomorrow is thrown into the oven, will he not much more clothe you—you of little faith?" (Matt. 6:25-30)

This kind of hope, which is (as I said) "in God" and not in ourselves, doesn't make anyone smug, neither does it detract from personal responsibility. It is not automatic, not a law of nature or history, that good shall come out of evil, or that present suffering will lead to ultimate rejoicing. Remember: we are talking about *faith*, not "sight"—about walking toward our destiny, not having arrived. So complacency is ruled out.

As for turning such hope into an excuse for doing nothing oneself, that would be a complete misunderstanding—a cheapening of the whole thing. The Spirit of God fosters hope in our hearts, not to preserve us from foresight and planning and hard work, but, on the contrary, in order to give us the kind of courage we need to believe that *our* work, which is never very great, is nevertheless enfolded in a more perfect work—God's "providential" governance of the world—and that our work is therefore contributing to the world's "mending" (to use a wonderful Jewish expression).

You know—yes, I think you already know this—how easy it is for us humans to become discouraged about the significance of our own efforts. Whether we are trying to build a house or raise a family or play a concerto or write a book, we are often assailed by feelings of self-doubt and the futility of our efforts. I confess to you: whenever I sit down to attempt, as I am doing right now, to explain something truly immense and profound—such as the nature of Christian hope—I have to do battle with little whisper-ings of my mind that mock my poor attempts: "What makes you think you can do justice to this? Why do you imagine your words can persuade anybody of anything?" And then I have to say to myself: "But my work, unimpressive as it may be, is only a small part of the visible tip of a labor—God's labor—that is infinitely greater. Moreover," I add, "this is the work to which I have been beckoned. God permits it, and God will do with it what God wills. So please, my dear sir: Get on with it!"

I'm trying to illustrate for you, once again out of my own life and experience, the difference that hope makes. It won't be quite the same for anybody else. You, for instance, are closer to the beginning of your journey than I am, and I suspect that one is able to be a little more confident about the effectiveness of Christian hope after years of relying upon it than when one is just starting out. I also recognize and take very seriously the fact that I belong to a generation that had a lot of history, so to speak, going for it, while you are part of "Generation X"—which may or may not be as jeopardized by time as people say. For you, the leap toward faith and hope may indeed be a greater leap than the one that people of my cohort were asked to take.

All the same, I know that the life force is strong in you. The very life within you, your will-to-live, will know how to recognize the gift of hope when it is offered you. And it will know, too, how to distinguish true hope from false or deceptive forms of hope. One should never, I think, give in too easily to any scheme or system that promises the victory of "the brighter side." Bargain with all such offers of hope, including—perhaps especially—the religious ones! The test that they must meet if they are to be worthy of your trust is this: "Am I allowed to keep my eyes wide open if I buy into this scheme, or must I close them and ... make a wish?" Only trust the offers that insist you keep your eyes wide open. Christian hope, unless it is turned into pious, sentimental optimism, does insist on that. After all, at its center is a cross!

Do you think, now, that I need to say anything about "the greatest of these"—love? Don't we all know, however hiddenly, that what makes the most difference is love? We know this when we are not loved, and we know it when we are. Every little concrete experience of loving or being loved confirms it. As a popular song of my youth (Victor Herbert's "Ah! Sweet Mystery of Life") summed the matter up, "It is love and love alone the world is seeking." Somewhat later in time, the Beatles told us that "All you need is love." So is it even necessary to talk about it, to explain the difference love makes—to "theologize"?

In a way, it isn't necessary. Something within us almost automatically responds to the biblical statement that "God is love" (1 John 4:8), or that best-known of all newer Testament statements, "God so loved the world that he gave his only son ..." (John 3:16). When Jesus summarized the whole law and the prophets by saying that there were only two commandments, and really only one, since the two are not separable (Mark 12:31: "Hear, O Israel: the Lord our God, the Lord is one; you shall love the Lord your God with all your heart, and with all your soul, and with all your mind, and with all your strength. The second is this, "You shall love your neighbor as yourself." There is no other commandment greater than these."), he could count on a certain readiness in his hearers to receive such a commandment—and to receive it, not just as a command, a prescription, but as a *description* of what we already know deeply. For God has created us for love, and, as St. Augustine said, we are "restless" until we know ourselves to be loved, and love in return.

On the other hand . . . (have you noticed?—there's always an "on the other hand" when one tries to speak about God, and humankind, and whatever is really *real*). So: on the other hand it *is* necessary to talk about love, if one wants to do justice to the Christian understanding of it. And the reason is that there is hardly anything in the world of our experience today that is so *mis*understood as love. I've said that both faith and hope are misunderstood, but the misunderstandings of love in our society are far more serious. And if we want to describe the difference love makes when it is understood in a Christian way we have to distinguish it from many of the assumptions about love that are at work in our culture, including religious assumptions.

For far too many of our contemporaries, love is almost just another word for sex. Everybody talks about "making love"—which, contrary to the older English uses of that term, has simply come to mean engaging in sex. Many in your generation seem not even to comprehend "romantic" love, so that when they look at old films or read nineteenth-century novels they find all the talk and gestures and agonizings of young lovers pretty comical, if not plain ridiculous. Why don't they just hop into bed with one another?— which is what the heros and nonheros of present-day films and novels seem invariably (I would say even boringly!) to do.

Don't misunderstand me: Christianity is not against sex, nor is it against all the passion that goes with love. It is fashionable in some quarters today to blame Christians, especially "the Puritans," for every sexual taboo and hang-up. That habit stems from a combination of historical ignorance and the tendencies of some Christian groups (not necessarily the Puritans, by the way) to reduce "sin" to so-called sins of the flesh and to put far too much emphasis on "the spirit" or "soul" over against the body. But at base, and certainly in its Hebraic roots, Christianity not only acknowledges but celebrates the creaturely, psychosomatic (spirit-body) unity of the human person. It isn't accidental that the Lord God in the saga of creation tells the human pair that he expects them to "be fruitful and multiply" (Gen. 1:28). The Creator didn't have to say that to the other creatures, but the humans needed to hear it—perhaps because the Bible already understood the strange temptation of human beings to try to escape from their bodies. (Or to reproduce by less messy, more predictable means? As in cloning?)

But while it is very positive about our sexuality, Christianity, when it is true to its own best traditions, does not elevate sex above its rightful place. And its *rightful* place is not where our society as a whole tends to put it: at the top! We are not just sex machines. The worth and meaning of our lives is not measured by our capacity for sexual expression. Neither heterosexuality nor homosexuality nor bisexuality nor any other conceivable sexual "orientation" defines our personhood! Sexy people are not more treasured by God than nonsexy people! And so on.

In fact, responsible *human* (not only Christian) sensibility today should be directed toward something like dethroning the bogus god, Sex. Of all the gods human imagination and desperation have between them concocted, sex as divinity is the most pathetic—and also the least merciful. In its place, sex is both necessary and pleasurable—so are eating and sleeping and exercising and many other physical activities that our minds and spirits require as much as do our bodies, to which they are united. But when any of these activities become the governing passion of our lives they can literally destroy us, and today many have been and are being destroyed, quite literally, by sex. So let's be wary of all the clever, seductive, and alluring promotion of sex, most of it crassly commercial at bottom, that makes it seem so wonderful and desirable and fails to mention that it is also full of destructive potential—a potential that is not, by the way, limited to the dangers of sexually transmitted diseases!

Love, as Christian faith understands it, may certainly entail sexual expression; and sexuality apart from love, while by no means the greatest sin imaginable, is not recommended. But in spite of this connectedness of sex with love, love as Christianly conceived is something far more inclusive than, and qualitatively distinguishable from, its sexual *expressions*. Some of the greatest lovers in human history, including some regarded by Christians as saints, never engaged in sexual relations or tried to refrain from doing so. When love is too exclusively associated with relationships in which sexual expression is expected, whole classes of human beings are excluded from love—or rather, from what love is reputed to mean. In the not-distant past, for instance, generations of "spinsters" and "bachelors" (as single women and men used to be called) were relegated to second-class humanity because they were sexually unattached. And if we think that such assumptions have been banished by our sexually "liberated" civilization, consider our existing attitude toward the elderly, the handicapped, the infirm, and those who for religious or other reasons deliberately choose a celibate life. In a real sense, the most pathetic of the many pathetic things about our contemporary culture is its tendency to equate love and sex. Far from being "liberated," such an equation amounts to one of the most absurd forms of oppression to which human beings have submitted—all the more absurd because it is largely self-imposed.

Sentimentalization of love

But there is also another kind of misunderstanding, where love is concerned, that is probably just as dreadful. I call it the sentimentalization of love. Love becomes "luv"—if you know what I mean. Next time you are in a so-called drugstore that sells so-called greeting cards (as drugstores for some odd reason must all do now!), spend a little time reading through the messages that these displays suggest we should send one another through the mail, and on every occasion from birth until death and beyond! Then you will understand what I mean by the sentimentalization of love.

What's involved is elementary, really: To turn love into "luv" you eliminate from love everything that seems ambiguous or dark or negative: you omit to mention that love profoundly challenges our self-centeredness; you don't remind people that the commitment that goes with real love is real *commitment.* You certainly don't hint that genuine relationships of love contain a high degree of honesty and the readiness to confront differences. And above all you never suggest that (to quote a phrase!) "the line between love and hate is as thin as a razor's edge." *Never* will you find that sentiment or anything remotely resembling it on a greeting card!

But you will find it in the Bible—for instance, it is all through the book of Proverbs. Because love, biblically understood, means first of all the determination of the loving God to enter into the very depths of human alienation and estrangement. God's love (you'll remember that we had to use that special word for it, earlier: *agape*)[5] is neither erotic love, as in some of the old nature religions, nor is it sentimentality. When the newer Testament, following the older Testament's insistence upon "divine pathos and compassion," comes straight out with the definition "God *is* love" (1 John 4:8), it does not mean that "God" is just a name for greeting card "luv" raised to the highest degree! God's love must be a love that suffers because those beloved by God—ourselves!—are very hard to love. We resist love—God's love, but also the love of others. Love is perhaps "all you need"—is what "the world is seeking"—but we run away from it at the same time as we want to run toward it.

Do you know what I mean? If you don't, then maybe you haven't yet experienced real love. But I'm sure you have, in fact, and that you do understand. Why do adolescents behave in the way that they do in relation to their parents? Why do brides and grooms, on the very eve of their weddings, give vent to bleak thoughts? Why, in every really loving relationship, is there always an element, however hidden and unexpressed, of resentment against the dimensions of commitment and concern that are imposed on one because of love?

The whole problematic of love is downplayed or simply unheard-of by love's sentimentalizers. *Of course* I would like to be loved and ᵥto love unambiguously, wholeheartedly! I would be overjoyed if love were all "yes" and no "no," all "come hither" and no "go away." But when I try to pretend that this is so, I give the lie to life—and, in the process, probably, impose enormous burdens of pretense and exaggeration on those who are the recipients of my love. I doubt it would be untrue to say that most of the marriage failures in our society are directly or indirectly related to our great social dishonesty about the darker, ambiguous side of love—which is dark and ambiguous, not because love is dark and ambiguous, but because we are. So if I called the sentimentalization of love "dreadful," I was not just being flippant. The cheapening of love in this way results in incalculable personal and societal costs.

But now I have said enough about what love is *not*, I hope, to make it possible to define love positively without indulging in easy generalizations and niceties. The defintion Paul gives in that passage I cited at the beginning can't be improved upon, I suspect. You should read it again and again. Remember, as you do, that Paul is describing in the first place God's love—and therefore neither our own actual loves nor a mere ideal. The whole presupposition of his so-called "hymn to love" is God's love as it is revealed and exemplified in Jesus as the Christ; so it is not really a hymn to *love*, properly speaking, but a hymn to God. The love that is "patient . . . kind . . . not envious or boastful or arrogant or rude . . . not irritable or resentful . . . rejoices in the truth . . . bears all things . . . endures all things" is that love with which "God so loved the world that he gave. . . ."[6]

That divine love, unmotivated by any gain for itself or any need in itself, is the background and necessity upon which our human love is to be grounded. So that when both Jesus and Paul (Rom. 13:9) speak of love as the commandment in which all the requirements of God are summed up, they are not speaking only of a commandment. As I have said before, and as every child knows, love can't be commanded in the first place. When the Bible "commands" us to love, it assumes that love is a real possibility for us, in spite of everything we put in its way, *because* we are already loved by God. As once again the great biblical poet of love, John, puts it: "We love because God first loved us" (1 John 4:19).

The love into which the divine Spirit is always seeking to draw our lives is a love that reflects God's love for us; therefore I have had to say that it is not to be equated with erotic or sexual love, and neither is it to be sentimentalized. God's love is extended to human beings without any regard for their sexuality, and it is extended to . . . sinners! And sinners, in this biblical language, does not mean people who are obviously or notoriously wicked, it means people whose relationships (with God, with one another, with the natural world) are all askew—alienated, estranged people. We are all such sinners, and as such we are a very hard lot to love—not so much because we are "bad" (most of us aren't that bad!) as because we are so centered in ourselves. We may "love" ourselves too much, or too little; in the end it comes to the same thing—our inordinate consciousness of *ourselves*. We have to be taken out of ourselves, shown the wide world that God has prepared for us like a garden, introduced to the others. We resist this. It seems to rob us of our independence, and how we North Americans treasure independence! But it is nonetheless the character of God's love to invade the very core of our selves, our inner sanctum, and turn us toward God and "the others."

And God deigns to do this, as I have said before in different ways, without just trampling upon us, stamping out our resistance, and *making* us love (which can't be done anyway). Rather, the divine Spirit achieves a beachhead of love within our suspicious hearts by allowing us to give full expression to our suspicion, our resistance, even our hatred. God's love, unlike sentimental love, does not intend that we should conceal or minimize all that; because it is only as "all that"—the suspicions, resistance, and hatred—are permitted to surface that we can know ourselves for what we are, and know that we are loved as we are.

It is all there, once again, in the cross of Jesus (see the Luther quotation in the previous footnote): that cross not only demonstrates the lengths to which God is ready to go in God's loving search for lost, alienated humanity; it also represents the grim extent of our human capacity to reject love when it is offered us. But it is precisely in this altogether honest confrontation of God and estranged humanity that real love begins to be learned.

I said *begins*! Let's not exaggerate that, either. If we do, we'll just end up with sentimentality again. No human love, Christian or otherwise, is perfect. At weddings in my youth, a favorite song used to be "O Perfect Love." The "perfect" love named in this song was in fact God's love; but in the context of the "pretty wedding" (as you called them earlier) everybody thought the song was celebrating the "perfect love" of the young couple—which was of course never perfect! Our loves are always only pale approximations, at best, of God's "*suffering* love"; and Christians more than anybody else should know this, because the "sin" they are supposed to confess *chiefly* is their perennial failure to love as they are loved.

Nevertheless, it is a beginning; and it does "make a difference." It makes the difference between confusing love with sex, and it makes the difference between love and "luv"—as I've argued here. But these are only two of the unlistable differences that love makes, and most of them we already know—not, maybe, with our heads, but in our hearts. We may not be able to speak about these differences, but we all are pretty adept at recognizing them when we see them.

Recognizing, for instance, the difference between a calculating sort of love that is all the time conscious of what it can get out of loving and, on the other hand, a love that "does not insist on its own way." Recognizing the difference between a love that is warm and glowing during the first five years of marriage and one that "never ends." Recognizing the difference between a love that is very conscious of itself loving, and one that "rejoices in the truth"—the truth, the integrity of the other. Recognizing the difference between a love that thinks it has become perfect and one that knows it is only in its childhood phase, only seeing and knowing "in part."

What difference can love—this kind of love—make in your life? That you must answer yourself.

I think you already know—"in part"—the answer.

Why Church?
(And by the Way, What about "The Others"?)

s i x

"I went to church again on Sunday," you announced as soon as you'd settled down in my old easy chair.

"That makes—what?—three times in the past month? You're becoming more regular in your church attendance than most members of the churches are! And what did you discover this last time?"

"Yes, what did I discover?... Well, this time it was a very 'Protestant' sort of service, I guess. I suppose you'd say 'liberal Protestant.' Or maybe 'conventional Protestant'? Anyway, it was quite different from the service I attended three weeks ago—the one with so much kneeling and set prayers and clergy in colorful robes and so on.

"It was also different from the 'evangelical' service I attended the week before. That one was certainly Protestant if Protestant means putting a lot of emphasis on Bible texts and sermons; but even from the little I know about the Protestant Reformation I doubt if Luther or Calvin would have felt at home there. So much depended on emotional involvement, and on having what seemed to me an almost superstitious reverence for the Bible, that I couldn't feel part of it—though I believe that most of the people there were really sincere. I suppose sincerity counts for something, even if it's misguided."

"What about the people at the liberal Protestant service yesterday," I asked, "were they ... sincere?"

"Maybe," you answered. "It was hard to tell. They didn't show much evidence of rapt involvement in what was going on. Their faces, which were pleasant enough on the whole, remained rather blank—well, perhaps that's too harsh. To be fairer I'd have to say that they didn't seem to be . . . moved, or deeply affected, one way or another. They were nice enough to one another, and one or two even spoke to me afterward, though I was a perfect stranger. They invited me to their coffee hour. I can't say they were unfriendly or anything. Only . . . well, I think they were more interested in one another, or (how to put it?) in just being there, than in anything that went on in the service itself."

"And what 'went on' in the service? I assume there was a sermon? How did it strike you?"

"Oh, yes, there was a sermon—I expected that. It was o.k. I don't remember it in detail, but it was about being . . . 'inclusive'—yes, that was the word that kept cropping up. I think it was even part of the title of the sermon given in the leaflet we all received. The preacher wanted us to be 'inclusive.' Too much that goes on in our society excludes others—whole groups like races and sexes, gays, women. Even religion, even Christianity, is often exclusive. But real Christianity teaches us to be inclusive. Actually, he frequently used the word 'love'—I think there was a text from one of Paul's letters, but not the one you wrote about last time; something about there being neither slave nor free, male nor female. . . .

"Well, it wasn't bad, you know. There were a couple of very good lines. People chuckled once or twice—so I suppose that's a form of being moved."

I was listening to all this with considerable interest. You were talking, as we both knew, about my own church—I mean, a congregation of my denomination. Evidently you were not put off by the experience. At the same time, it was pretty plain that you were holding something back, and I wanted to find out what it was. I decided on the direct approach.

"What bothered you about this service?" I asked.

Your answer was a long time in formulating itself, but this, I think, is how it came out: "I'm probably too critical, but I had the impression that God wasn't very real for those nice people. It was all very matter-of-fact, if you know what I mean. There wasn't much mystery about the service. With that formal service I attended earlier—the one with the processions and all—one felt at least the external trappings of mystery. Maybe that, too, was just conventional—the regular thing, you know, for those particular people. But, to be honest, I'd have difficulty distinguishing the Protestant service yesterday from many other sorts of public meetings."

"And the sermon? Was it a sort of lecture?"

"Not exactly a lecture. More like a pep talk. As I said, the main point was that we were being urged to be 'inclusive.' Actually, I felt that everybody present agreed with that beforehand. I could almost hear them saying, 'No problem.' Whether they actually behaved inclusively, I don't know of course. But personally, you know, I began to feel a little uncomfortable with that message."

"Why was that?"

"Well, I haven't figured that out for myself yet, but it seems to me there's a problem that the preacher was not being very honest about. Maybe it wasn't a problem for him, but it seems to me to be a problem all the same. I mean, if you're a Christian—if you really believe that Jesus (to use your language) is the one who makes God 'particular,' 'concrete,' then haven't you already opted for something that excludes others? Isn't there an excluding element in any *religion, in fact—or for that matter in any system of thought, like Platonism, or Marxism, or whatever—even 'New Age'?*

"Sure, well-mannered, friendly people of any religious or philosophical or political persuasion can be 'inclusive' in their behavior toward others. But isn't there an element of exclusivity in any point of view as such, *including Christianity? And I think my problem with the sermon was that the preacher didn't seem to recognize that. Maybe most of the people listening didn't, either. Is it just my twisted mind, or is there some kind of contradiction here?"*

"What you're saying, I guess, is that you didn't sense in the preacher's exhortation to inclusivity any indication of the basis *on which Christians could and should be inclusive. Would that be it?"*

"*Perhaps. Partly. What strikes me (am I wrong?) is that there is a problem for Christians here. And I don't think you can solve it by just telling people they should love everybody—be inclusive. Is love itself . . . 'inclusive'? I've been in love a couple of times, or so I thought, and I recall a rather hugely exclusive element in it: I chose that person and not . . . 'everybody.' A couple of individuals who would have been pleased enough had I chosen them definitely felt excluded! There were some definite problems over that, I remember. If Christians choose Jesus Christ (why would they be Christians otherwise?), what are they going to do about all the people who don't choose Jesus Christ, or maybe don't even know the name?*"

"*What would you gather about the other churches you attended? What answer would they give to that question?*"

"*I expect,*" you answered, "*that the formal church people don't think much about that. I imagine they're content just to be who they are and do what they do. As for the evangelicals, I have the definite impression (not just from that one service but from other things I know about them) that they're not very inclusive at all. They're pretty up front, in fact, about Jesus being 'the only way.'*"

"*And what would you yourself prefer, when it comes to this problem?*"

"*That's easy—or is it? I certainly don't want to belong to any outfit that shuts out whole great gobs of humanity—and in advance! . . . All the same, if I'm going to give myself to anything—religion or whatever!—I want it to be something I can consider significant and decisive enough to claim my commitment. And, frankly, I couldn't get excited enough about the sort of Christianity I witnessed last Sunday to feel it had any great claim on me. Maybe it was just too familiar, too predictable. I'm part of the middle class myself, as you know, so I found nothing surprising or unusual in that service of worship. By the same token, there was nothing challenging, either. At no point did I feel . . . well, touched, or moved. Or even specially interested.*"

"*So I suppose,*" I said, "*that the problem you're posing for me could be put this way: 'Is there any Christianity that takes seriously the particularity of its own confession and is at the same time able,* through *that confession, to be hospitable to those who do not make that confession?"*

You thought about that for a few seconds, and then you more or less agreed with that way of formulating the question. "But," you added, "there's one question that I'd put before that one; and it's this: Is the church necessary in the first place? Isn't the church itself a large part of the problem? I mean, if you institutionalize something like Christianity haven't you just added complications to an already complicated problem? People who are loyal to ideas, or beliefs, or systems of thought are already begging the question about 'the others'; but people who are loyal to institutions—*religious or otherwise; nations, for instance*—have an extra reason for excluding other people. The institution itself promotes a sense of the 'otherness' of those who don't belong to it. If churches were done away with, wouldn't the lines of distinction between Christians and 'the others' be a little less . . . well, distinct? And I have to ask anyway, on the basis of what we've been discussing about Christianity as a whole: Is the church—not to mention all the different churches!—really necessary?"

Again we tried to wrestle with those questions of yours—and again we parted without feeling, either one of us, that we'd done the questions justice. Obviously, they are questions that one has to live with for a long time. My professorial compulsion to answer everything drove me to my desk soon after I got home that evening, however, and I produced once more—"for your consideration," so to speak—a little essay.

The Churches, the Church, and the "Realm of God"

I am going to assume for purposes of ordering our thought that there are two questions requiring response here: (1) Is the church necessary? and (2) What about all the people who aren't part of the Christian church? As you rightly hinted at the end of our conversation, the two questions aren't really separable; in the end they converge. But let's think about them separately first, and as we go along we'll gradually discover, I think, their connectedness.

Is the church necessary?

Let me warn you in advance that I'll have to answer "Yes" to that. But if my affirmative answer is going to carry any weight with you, I think, I'll once again have first to clear away some debris—some misunderstandings and false impressions. There is a great deal of such debris surrounding this subject. I even hesitate to get into it with you. So much of it is "our" problem—I mean, a problem (or rather, a whole bag of problems) that we who continue to belong to the churches and have leadership in them have to sort out. It shouldn't be loaded onto the shoulders of people like you, who are just on the edges of this faith, looking in. But unless I make some distinctions and observe some facts of history I'm afraid I would just be guilty of misleading you. I could tell you all the good reasons I know why the church is necessary, and you might even agree with them. But then as soon as you tried to check out such reasoning by associating with actual, existing congregations, as you've begun to do, you would likely be disappointed.

This leads me directly to the first observation (there will be three of them) that I want to make by way of clearing away some of the debris.

It's this: *When we think about the church, we should try to avoid being idealistic, romantic, utopian.* The same thing would have to be said about any institution, really, including universities. But for some reason people expect churches to avoid all the problems that beset other institutions. It isn't so. Wherever there are imperfect people, there will be imperfect organizations; and wherever the imperfect people try to be honest and intimate (as churchfolk often *do* try) the imperfections of their community may be even more visible than elsewhere.

There is no such thing as a "perfect" church, and the people who go about looking for such an ideal are bound to be disappointed. The Christian gospel isn't about the perfect church, it's about the perfect love of God, which none of us deserves, and from which we all fall short. The church is not a little bit of the world that has finally been fixed up, righted. In a real way, the only thing that distinguishes church and world is that the church knows something about the world that it doesn't usually know about itself: that it is greatly loved. Loved, and therefore also judged. You could say (the biblical letter of Peter does!) that the church is the place where God's loving judgment of the world begins (1 Peter 4:17). God wants to strip away the falseness and suspicion and pretense and hypocrisy of human beings in their relating to one another, and have them encounter one another as they really are—as creatures of God who share the same problems and possibilities. What we call "church" is nothing more nor less than a small beginning in the direction of becoming real.

It's only a beginning—oh, the beginning of a beginning of a beginning! Remember, we're talking about a people who are "on the way," who haven't "arrived." Every day they start the journey over again, remembering that they've deviated from the route often enough before, and so not pretending to know *exactly* where they are, and certainly not presuming they're going to arrive inevitably and unscathed at their destination. If they relied on their own past experience, or their expertise as "travelers," they would soon give up the journey. But they do not trust in themselves; they trust the One who said, "Follow me." So, hesitantly, hoping against hope (Rom. 4:18), they are able to go on, despite the hardships, the discouragements, the in-fighting, and the vicissitudes of historical existence.

To expect such a community "in transit" to be perfect, as if it had already attained its final destination, is to demonstrate how naive one is about the whole business of living by faith, not sight—what we talked about before. *One should assume that there will be something wrong with the church.* Not one of the biblical letters of Paul and the others to those little communities of Christians in the Mediterranean world of long ago lacks an element of implicit or explicit criticism. They all presuppose that the Christian communities have a long way to go. And even when some of the shortcomings are corrected, others crop up and have to be pointed out. We have to face it: the church never has got it right and never is going to get it all right.

But don't be tempted by that insight to jump into the opposite danger! Just because "church" already implies imperfection, misappropriation of the truth, and downright sin, it should not be imagined that we've just got to live with that—adjust, so to speak, to the perennial wretchedness of the churches. The newer Testament's letters to the churches, including the pithy little letters in the book of Revelation (chapters 2 and 3), all (as I said) assume that something will be wrong. But they also assume that *some* of what is wrong can be changed, and must be. That's why there is this relentless apostolic harping on ecclesiastical problems in these letters: because many of these problems don't have to be. There are other possibilities. Perfection will never be reached—not as *church*, anyway. But some things are better than others—better, because nearer to the "travel plan," so to speak, laid out by the one the Bible sometimes calls our "Pioneer" (Heb. 12:2).

The distinction I'm making here is of course not an easy one to observe always. People who are really committed to the church (and despite my reputation in some quarters, I am one of them!) are often chided by their co-Christians for being too critical. Perhaps we critics *are*, sometimes, in danger of being perfectionists, who want the church to measure up to some impossible ideal. But usually, I think, the insider critics of the churches are just carrying on the biblical tradition of recalling the people of God to their rightful identity and vocation. That, at least, is what I've understood to be my own Christian calling, as a theologian. I am far from being a perfectionist when it comes to the Christian church. But I'm absolutely convinced that some of the things that are wrong with the churches today can be changed—and indeed that they must be changed, if we are ever going to become worthy of our identity with that Pioneer.

So, my second and third little exercises in debris-clearing will be about some of those necessary changes.

Second, then, *"the church" is not to be equated with "the churches" or with whatever happens to call itself "church."* I like a line of St. Augustine's: "Many whom God has, the church does not have, and many whom the church has God does not have."[1]

In other words, the identity of what we call Christ's "church"— who belongs to it, who doesn't—is a mystery known only to God. It is not something that human wisdom or human authority has at its disposal. Some very staunch churchgoers *may* in fact be far from membership in Christ's church, whereas some people on the edges of the faith—people like you, for instance—may be closer to the center than they themselves realize. Here, too, Christians must live with the mystery stated by Jesus when he said that the first may be last and the last first (Matt. 19:30; Mark 9:35; 10:31; and others).

I suppose this is a particularly "Protestant" understanding (though Augustine was no Protestant, of course!), but it is both biblical and part of the greater tradition of Christian thought. The Reformers didn't *invent* the distinction between what they called "the church visible" and "the church invisible." That was their language, to be sure, but it reflects a much more extensive distinction that reaches back into the long tradition of Jerusalem. The prophets of ancient Israel were always drawing on this distinction, when they reminded people that there should be no *presumption* where God is concerned. The test of "belonging," so far as human capabilities go, is faithfulness, neither ancestry nor external observances nor mere words. Jesus summarized this prophetic test when he said, "By their fruits you will know them" (Matt. 7:16).

And the "fruits" he was talking about were ethical, mainly. There are lots of people who know all the right answers to doctrinal questions, who pray according to "the rules," and who observe ecclesiastical rituals impeccably and are not part of God's "kingdom" or "realm," for they neglect those who most need their help. Their speech may be brimming with religious references; they may go about talking about "the Lord" a good deal, as Jesus put it; but because they don't see "the Lord" in the faces of the poor and needy right in their midst their religious piety is not authentic. On the other hand, there are people who never heard of "the Lord," or do not acknowledge him, but who, because they love and serve others really belong to God's realm without knowing it (see Matt. 25:31-46).

"Church," in other words, is a very big idea. It is not to be reduced to petty, institutional concepts and precepts, rules and regulations, membership rolls and baptismal records and church givings! "Church" is not a club, and certainly not a whole lot of mutually suspicious and competetive clubs! In fact, as I may have pointed out to you before, in the beginning Christians didn't talk much about "the church"; they considered themselves "people of the Way"—by which they meant the Way of Jesus, the Way of the Cross, the *Via Dolorosa*. And, as I keep reminding you, to think of oneself as being "on the way," *en route*, so to speak, is at the same time to admit quite openly that one has not arrived at one's destination. About the destination they were agreed: they called it God's kingdom, God's realm or reign, the eternal life that God intends for God's people.[2] But they did not identify *themselves*— that is, they did not equate "the church"—with that realm. With them, too, there could be no presumption; and Paul, as well as Jesus, took up the whole Hebrew prophetic motif and reminded his little congregations very often that they should not, as we might say, count their chickens before they hatch! All our "ancestors," he said (and he meant our Jewish fathers and mothers of old), were part of the exodus from Egypt, but none of those who left Egypt managed to enter the promised land (1 Cor. 10:1ff.)!

What we have in the newer Testament by way of a concept of "church" is in fact far removed from the notion of "institution." The first Christians were not thinking in institutional terms at all, they were thinking in terms of a *movement*. A movement, any movement, has to be *organized*, of course. If you ask people involved in the peace movement today, or ecological movements, or the women's movement, they will tell you that organization is necessary. But they will also probably tell you that the great *danger* to any movement is exactly the danger of its becoming *over-organized, that is, institutionalized.*

Institutionalization means the hardening of the organizational forms necessary to movement, or of some of them. It happens easily and often unnoticed. Some organizational ideas appear to "work," or are considered essential by certain powerful elements within the movement, so they are given a sort of permanence ("We've always done it in this way!"). These methods were adopted in the first place because they met the needs of the moment, of this time and this place; but in their hardened, institutionalized form they are believed to be permanently correct and necessary— mandatory for every time and every place. Such institutionalized theories and methods become self-perpetuating, creating their own need for continuance, often without regard to what is *actually* needed. Certain offices or administrative positions are thought to be essential and unchangeable; buildings become very significant; bureaucracies are created. And when this happens to religious organizations, including Christianity, all of these phenomena are provided with an aura of "the eternal" supposedly based on God's own design, so that the usual "human" logic of the transition from movement to institution is, in the *religious* organization, made even weightier by its reputation for being part the very Plan of God.

And you are quite right: this institutional business does complicate the whole question of "the others." When Christians are no longer just "Christians" or "People of the Way," but Presbyterians, Anglicans, Lutherans, Methodists, Roman Catholics, and so on, those who do not "belong" to the denomination in question are all the more "other." In fact, as we know very well on this continent, with the proliferation of Christian denominations the list of those who are "other" swells to include not only members of other religious faiths but other *Christians*, whose "church" is not quite legitimate from the points of view of ecclesiastical institutions whose doctrines and practices differ.

This brings me to the *third* deposit of debris that must be cleared away before we can speak reasonably about the church's "necessity." We've had some occasion to think about it already, so I won't have to dwell on it extensively. I'm referring to the Big Change that occurred in the form and function of the Christian movement in the fourth century C.E., when under the emperors Constantine the Great and Theodosius the Great Christianity was made the official religion of the Roman Empire. What we need to notice about this transition so far as our present theme is concerned is that *the political establishment of Christianity in the fourth century C.E. made the tendency toward institutionalization infinitely greater than it had been in the preestablished state of the movement.*

This was inevitable, I believe. No empire is going to adopt as its own favored religious cult something as fluid and unstructured and organizationally adaptable as the church of the earliest centuries was. I'm not overlooking the fact that some types of organization had already hardened before the Roman Empire became interested in Christianity. But surely it must be obvious to everyone that a religion that is invited to come into the king's house, so to speak, and be chaplain to the whole realm—that such a religion is going to have to conform in some pretty basic ways to the organizational structures already "in place" within the realm.

And Rome, as we know, was extremely well organized. So it is not accidental that the Christian church increasingly reflected in its own organization the governance of the Empire itself, with a parallel "emperor" at its head (the pope), a hierarchy of bishops and lesser clergy (similar to provincial governors and local administrators), and so on. In fact, wherever Christianity has aligned itself with some imperial, national, or dominant social structure, it has tended to reflect in its own set-up the organizational patterns of its host society. That is what "establishment" means. The church becomes part of the "establishment" by adapting both its message and its structure to the already-established patterns of its host culture.

So it's not surprising that the church you attended on Sunday, like most of the older Protestant churches, reflects the organizational patterns of the business and professional world in our democratic, modified-capitalist system. If you got to know the workings of that denomination, you would hear people talking about their "head office," and "secretaries," and "committees," and "national budgets," and many other things that are also associated with secular corporations. In their forms of government and administration, these churches are telling themselves, their members, and the public at large that they really are part of the society—the religious part, to be sure, but quite compatible with all the other parts. So people can go to church without feeling they've entered a different sphere. That's why you yourself felt, if not "at home" exactly, at least on familiar ground, being yourself, as you said, part of "the middle class."

What we have to notice about this kind of Christian "establishment" is that in the process something is nearly always lost. What is lost? One way of answering that is to say that the dimension of difference or distinctiveness has been lost. There is nothing surprising, unusual, strange. This is why you thought you could almost hear that liberal congregation, in response to the preacher's insistence on inclusivity, intoning, "No problem." It is also why you yourself sensed throughout the service a sort of familiarity with everything. There were no surprises for you. And there were no challenges, either. This is not accidental. The "established" church can ask people to believe more fervently what they already believe, or to follow still more diligently the moral codes they already (at least rhetorically) honor; but it cannot introduce a "message" that is really different, new, and quite possibly critical of the values and mores its adherents hold. Rather, if and when it does that, it will inevitably alienate some of its customary clientele.

So far as the structure of the church is concerned, what is lost in highly institutionalized Christianity is inevitably the movement-quality of the biblical church. As the word *established* itself suggests, in the established church it is precisely movement that has to be avoided. Most people do not want to belong to something that is moving, changing, in flux; they want to be part of something stable and stationary, steadfast, permanent. In fact, the establishment of religions is always partly the result of the human desire to have, in the midst of life's changes, something that seems solid and constant. That is why so many Christians today (and not only Christians) are upset by changes occurring in the churches.

But life *is* change; and when the churches refuse to change they always tend to cut themselves off from life. More importantly, they are likely to cut themselves off from the living God, whose love toward the world requires constant attention to the here and now. What is *really* permanent, in the biblical understanding of this, is not temples and churches and liturgies and doctrines and hymnbooks, but God's love. That is what faith relies on: whatever else happens, *God will love.* And the point is this: love, when it is real and steadfast, always has to be on the move, because it is addressed to beings—ourselves—who do not stand still, but constantly change.

So "movement" is not only a matter of the church's structure, it is bound up with its very message and mission. When the church opts for institutional forms that deny or impede movement, it is putting a stumbling block in the way of God's communication with the world. This is why the prophets of ancient Israel complained that when Israel "settled down" in "the promised land"— when, in their words, the wandering, exiled people of ancient

Israel exchanged their tents for houses—something happened to Israel: it tended to become smug and stagnant, self-satisfied, entrenched, inflexible. Like most property owners, established religion grows more concerned for maintaining itself than in being a people with a mission to others.

This, many would say, is precisely what happened to the Christian church when it exchanged its wandering, scattered (the technical word is *diaspora*), and never-quite-legal status prior to Constantine for the status of official religion. What we call "Christendom," that is, the dominance of the Christian religion (not of the Christ!), differs from the earlier forms of Christianity in the world chiefly by being highly institutionalized in ways reflective of the organization forms of successive Western empires, and so of tending to behave in imperialistic ways itself—for instance, vis-à-vis the non-Christian religions. (Think of the crusades against Islam. Think of the long history of the persecution of European Jewry; think of the pogroms, and of the other more subtle ways of excluding the Jews. Think of Auschwitz!).

That doesn't mean that nobody objected to Christianity's establishment. Throughout the sixteen or so centuries since this legalized establishment of Christianity in the fourth century, there have always been minorities in and around Western Christendom that attempted to recover the earlier, movement-quality of the disciple community. In some important ways, the monastic movement throughout Christian history has been part of that attempt; so, in its original phases, was the Reformation of the sixteenth century. Still, it has been extremely hard, in the past, for Christians to break out of the "Christendom" mold of the church; because Christendom was not only powerful, politically speaking, and therefore able to curb its dissident groups, but Christianity was so firmly established in the West as the only acceptable religion that even the dissident groups usually tended, in the end, to return to some variation on the theme of establishment.

For instance, in terms of its basic *theological* ideas and principles, the Reformation heralded by Wycliff and Hus and spearheaded a century later by Luther was radically antiestablishment. The terrible things that Luther said about the Roman Pope were not personal, really, they were uttered against a whole form of the church that in Luther's mind had become corrupt—and had become that way because it had gone after power for itself by prostituting itself with the powerful, and not remaining faithful to the weak, crucified Christ! Ironically, however, when the German princes took up Luther's cause, he found himself locked into the same kind of questionable relation to the powerful—only, of course, different powers.

Now, I've gone into all this history, not only because it is necessary (as I said) to clear away some of the debris, but because I want to make a still more important point about the present—and with this I am moving toward the positive answer I want to give to your question about the necessity of the church: In our time, we have arrived at a juncture in history when it is quite possible (I would say that it is absolutely necessary!) for the Christian faith to recover in a livelier and more profound way than has been possible for centuries precisely the *movement* quality that belongs to its biblical and best theological traditions. I've written about this in several places, and I'd be glad to know what you think of my arguments there.[3] But here, and for now, I just have time to say in passing what I mean by this new opportunity and necessity that confronts the churches and all Christians who are serious about their faith.

For at least two centuries now, there has been what we may think of as an unwinding or a dismantling of "Christendom." The whole "modern" period (that is to say, from the eighteenth century onward, particularly) has introduced an immense and lasting criticism of religion in general and Christianity in particular. Today, as I have said before, many people are having second thoughts about the possibility of getting along without God, or religion, but the questioning of all traditional forms of Christianity has not slackened in our time, it has even grown more intense. Because now, instead of having only the alternative of a nonreligious secularism, people have all kinds of non-Christian *religious* alternatives to choose from—all the way from quite definitive forms of Islam, for instance, to vague types of "spirituality" like "New Age" and so forth. As I've said before, there are no longer great social currents and forces pushing people, generation after generation, into some Christian denomination or other. In fact, as you've noted yourself, congregations of Christians today are noticeably smaller and older, because the whole convention of passing church membership from parents to children has broken down.

I call this long process Christendom's "demise." Western Christendom (I am not talking about Christianity or the Christian faith, but about Christendom, that is, the cultural domination of the Christian religion) is virtually at an end, despite the fact that here and there, particularly in the U.S. south, it can seem to be alive and well. Although some like to point to increased church membership in Africa, Asia, and Latin America, the global picture does not in the least confirm the missionary idealism and zeal of certain Christian groups in North America, who still want to believe that they are going to make the whole world Christian very soon now. Meanwhile, the decline of Christendom in our midst has not gone unnoticed in most of the older, longer-established denominations; and here and there people are trying to be responsible and innovative about that great change. On the whole, however, the churches attempt, I think, to carry on "business as usual," and to do so as long as they can get away with it.

And just here we have to return to your experiences in the three churches whose services you have attended, particularly the last one—that "liberal Protestant" church, about which you told me more than about the other two.

I was intrigued by your whole report on that service. You shouldn't assume that your observations of one Sunday service give you the right to make vast generalizations. There are exceptions to what you experienced in that congregation—and even that congregation is undoubtedly more complex than your brief encounter with it could show. All the same, what you described was typical enough of many North American churches to warrant some serious reflection on the part of all who care about the future of the church on this continent.

What a strange combination of elements was present in what you told of that worship service! On the one hand, a sort of one-dimensional practicality, with no surprises, no enthusiasm, no challenges, and an air of ordinariness; on the other hand, obviously a need for some sort of public ritual, perhaps born of nostalgia, but also reflecting the desire for a meaningful community (which perhaps was better met by the coffee hour than by the service of worship itself). And added to that, it may well be, the keen observer could have detected some quiet search for personal meaning, for affirmation, maybe even for cleansing—but this, I think, at a mostly hidden level.

I'd like to help you interpret that experience, and the best way I can think of doing so is by asking you to think about it in the light of the "big picture" I've been painting here—the demise of Christendom. European Christians have been conscious of this demise for a long time, but it has caught us by surprise. Today the churches on our continent find themselves enmeshed in an immense transition for which they have neither precedent nor the theological criteria to assess. As Christendom draws to a close, what characterizes most of the formerly most-established churches of our society is a grand confusion. Although some of the more conservative, fundamentalistic and other Christian groups seem to flourish (not mainly, I think, for purely religious reasons), all of the once-major and long-established churches face unnerving declines in numbers, finances, and influence. Among churches in large cities in both Canada and the northern United States there is a sense of failure and impotence that is only barely covered by conventional expressions of optimism and positive thinking; and informed persons in all denominations know that even the apparently "successful" congregations have a question mark written over their future.

But, as we've observed already, human beings are famous for blotting out what they do not know how to come to terms with; and so long as the churches can give the appearance of "business as usual" they refrain from engaging in the sort of critical, imaginative thought that might make them interesting to people like you. You—quite rightly!—and not only you, but thousands like you, sense in and around these old, established churches of Christendom the aroma of decay. Rightly, you are looking for life, for meaning, for real community with others, and for some genuine sense of God's presence and care. But—yes, of course, with exceptions—you do not find it in these places. You yourself said it: "God does not seem to be very real to these nice people." This may be too harsh a judgment about many individuals and even groups within these churches, but I think it is not too harsh a judgment of what remains in our midst of "Christendom." Too many churches are so concerned about their own survival, yet so committed to maintaining the images of well-being they have always projected in our society, that they seem incapable of the kind of honest self-criticism that would be needed to meet the challenges of the day. They are trying very hard to keep Christendom alive—to put that Humpty Dumpty together again, as I sometimes express it. But if they would give up on such a futile project and ask seriously about the alternatives that *are* open to them just at this point in time they might be filled with new enthusiasm and new life that people like you would find very interesting, even exciting.

I am trying to be very honest with you. You aren't alone; people with your kinds of questions and concerns often find churches today less than helpful—to say it in the most charitable way I can. Still, you should try to understand that this is at least partly because our churches are going through the most difficult period, probably, of their entire history. They have inherited from the past a whole great mechanism—Christendom—that some of us would say *always* represented something like a basic misunderstanding of the church. And because they are so conditioned by that past, and so afraid of the unknown but likely radically different future, they can seem almost transfixed—like a frog caught within the predatory aura of a serpent.

But (and I hope you will take this very seriously) precisely because of their perilous, vulnerable, and uncertain situation, these churches (or many of them) are in a position to be influenced and changed by people who ask great questions, and who feel that somewhere, hidden in these old "earthen vessels" of churches, there could be some kind of "treasure" worth being unearthed. You are yourself such a person, or you are beginning to be. So if you can become knowledgeable enough and charitable enough to realize that the church is bigger than "the churches," you and like-minded people of your generation could become men and women who help Christianity find its way into *post-*Christendom forms that might really do something for the world that God loves.

Having said *that*, I have already affirmed implicitly that, "Yes, the church is necessary." There *is* a great treasure here, and it is not one that Christians can do without—or just bury in the ground, under a lot of . . . debris (Matt. 25:14-30)! The necessity of the church can be expressed positively in at least three ways:

It is necessary *first* of all because faith, which as we have seen before, "seeks understanding," also seeks community—what is called in the newer Testament *koinonia* (communion with others, participation). The very fact that you, with your big questions, have come so often to talk with me, is a small demonstration of what I mean. There is something in faith—even in its most initial stirrings, even when it may consist more of questions than of answers—that drives one to seek out others. Of course, the need for companionship is a basic human drive, and one that Christianity assumes. But faith looks for more than just company; it impels us to seek out others with whom we can share the joys and the agonies of faith's discoveries. Your evident disappointment with the worship service you attended yesterday is in part, I suspect, the result of your having failed to find in that place the possibility of such sharing. If you were to persist, you might still find that possibility there; because it is very likely that there are others like you also in that congregation. But of course you would have to work at it; and probably you are not in a position to do so just yet.

But let me go on with my reasons why "the church" is necessary: *Second*, behind the drive to communion with others that is in faith itself, there is the very nature of the Christian message to which faith is a response. For it is a message of *reconciliation*. That is, "gospel" is about the love of God, revealed through Christ, which reconciles us to all from which we have been estranged—not only God, but also other human beings and the creation itself. This is why Paul, in one of his famous summaries of the meaning of the Christian message, writes, "in Christ God was reconciling the world to himself, not counting their trespasses against them, and entrusting the message of reconciliation to us" (2 Cor. 5:19, NRSV).

It would be a very strange thing—a contradiction, in fact—if this "message of reconciliation" were to be announced by lone individuals who neither had nor desired any connections with one another. If reconciliation is what the Christian message is all about, and if there is any truth in that message, then it *must* express itself in a gathering of people who are reconciled to one another—or at least beginning to be. As it is, sadly enough, one of the most embarrassing things about the church is that it is so divided—that "it" is a "they," a plurality: churches. And not only churches, but churches that are often quite unreconciled to one another, mutually suspicious, and often visibly at odds. It is hardly a recommendation of the "message of reconciliation" when "the messengers" are themselves alienated from one another. For that reason, some of the best efforts of serious Christians in the present century have been devoted to the so-called "ecumenical movement," that is, the attempt to achieve a greater unity among Christian bodies that are historically divided. And this, too, will have to become an even greater endeavor in the twenty-first century. It is part of what is involved in finding new forms of the Christian movement in the post-Christendom situation. And it is possible, too, because much about the church's dividedness is clearly bound up with Christendom and the quest for power that Christendom entails. So another reason why the end of Christendom can be welcomed by serious Christians is that it can give the ecumenical movement a new and more vital future.

Which leads to my *third* positive response to your question whether the church is necessary. I've said its necessity comes from faith itself, and from the message to which faith is a response; and now I must add that the church's necessity lies also in its "necessary" mission to the world. And here we'll have to notice that the *two* questions we began with come together.

Christianity does have a mission to the world, and that mission is the most basic reason for the existence of the church. There are religions (some would claim that Judaism is one of them) that do not have a missionary impulse in them; but Christianity has been pushed out into the world from the beginning, like a little fledgling bird nudged out of its cozy nest by its parents. That is in fact a good simile, because what drives Christianity (as distinct from Christendom) towards the world is not personal eagerness for exposure to the public sphere, nor a desire to become big and powerful, nor a sense of its superiority over every other faith. No, it is "*sent* out" (that is what the word *apostolic* means), usually against its will, by the God who has called it into being, because of love for . . . *the world.*

That is a very important thing to remember when it comes to asking about "the others." The object of God's love, according to biblical faith, is not first of all the church; it is the world: "God so loved the *cosmos* . . ." (John 3:16; not accidentally, I think, that is the single best known verse of the newer Testament). The church is only a means to the end, not the end as such. The end—the goal that this faith envisages—is the "salvation" of the world (using "salvation" in the way we spoke of it earlier, that is, God wants to make the world whole, to fulfill its promise, to "mend" its torn and tattered life). Already with this quite fundamental assumption, then, one has to question the idea—an idea that some Christians certainly entertain—that only *bona fide* church members are eligible for salvation.

I'll come back to that in a moment. For now, I only want to point out that the mission of the church is of central importance to Christian faith, so much so that it constitutes the most basic reason why the church must exist. Of course the church needs to have periods of retreat from the world, to recover its own identity through study and prayer, to renew its courage, and so on. But precisely in these times of renewal, the church learns once more that it does not exist for its own sake. A church that hived off to itself and was content to be a comfortable "fellowship" would contradict in the most flagrant way the whole message of the New Testament.

Now already I can hear you complain, "But isn't this Christian sense of having a world mission precisely the source of Christian imperialism? Isn't it exactly that missionary zeal that lies behind all the militant and often violent behavior of Christians in relation to 'the others'?"

I respect this question; it's one that many people ask today. I know that it can not be answered easily or flippantly. Too much history over the past two millennia tells the story of a zealous, strident, judgmental religion that in the name of Jesus Christ tried to "conquer the world." And alas, the attempt has by no means come to an end! In fact, the year 2000, at the portal of which we are now standing, has again (as in 1000 C.E.) evoked in the hearts of many keen Christians the thought that new efforts have now to be made to bring the world to kneel before the Christ.

I want to make my position on this entirely clear: All that "conquering" business represents a gross—no, even a fantastic!—misunderstanding of both the gospel and the church's mission. Please consider me a Christian critic of all such religious zeal—and it is *religious* zeal. In fact it belongs to the essence of religion, as I have often used that term in our discussions here; for religion, as distinct from faith, is from beginning to end all about conquering—first conquering God, getting control of the Controller, as those poor builders of the Tower of Babel wanted to do (Genesis 11), and then conquering everybody else. Religion is always about power. Faith, on the contrary, is about love—and therefore weakness. Yes, weakness! For the only "power" that can commend love is from the vantage point of worldly ways sheer weakness—the weakness of serving others, of being ready to suffer for and with them, of considering them before oneself, patience, kindness . . . all those things that we read in Paul's "hymn to love."

As the revealer of God's love for the world, the way of worldly power and glory is denied Jesus. He is tempted to follow that way—that's what the temptations in the wilderness are all about (Luke 4:1-13), but he rejects it decisively. Unfortunately, ironically, Christendom took up with a certain enthusiasm the very temptations that Jesus resisted! Just consider what an astonishing contradiction is involved in the idea of conquering the world for Jesus Christ, the one who "laid down his life for his friends," who loved and forgave his enemies. Of course, if you turn Jesus Christ into some kind of a Caesar or Napoleon, the ultimate autocrat, you can indulge logically in such a "conquering" notion of the church's mission. And let's be honest: too often Jesus Christ has had precisely that image imposed on him! But it can only be done by very ignorant or deliberately deviant people—or, to be more accurate, by people whose own thirst for conquering outweighs their integrity as students of the Scriptures!

I suppose one shouldn't be too hard on those people. After all, the religious impulse with its drive to power is there in all of us. We all want to have the upper hand, be on the winning team. And we all know, too well, the temptation to secure our cause, whatever our cause may be, through sheer machismo and bravado—and wherever possible, "with God's help!" To turn Jesus Christ into the sort of conquering hero who could lead us into battle against all real and potential and imagined enemies was probably the most natural thing in the world. The Gospel writers were very familiar with that temptation. In fact, the one whom they (or at least subsequent history) regard as the chief apostle, Peter, is presented in the Gospels as a rough and ready type whose first thought is always some variation on the theme, "Conquer!" At one point he tells Jesus that if anybody thinks they're going to make Jesus suffer they'll have to do so (as he might have said today) "over my dead body" (Matt. 16:21-23). And when the soldiers come to capture Jesus on the Mount of Olives, it was Peter who whipped out his sword to defend his teacher (Luke 22:50f.)!

What is more significant still, is that whenever this conquering alternative is advanced in the Gospel accounts, not only in connections with Jesus' own temptations, Jesus rejects it, and usually in the strongest possible way. He even calls Peter demonic when Peter vows to prevent anyone from harming Jesus: "Get behind me, Satan!" (Matt. 16:23). And he not only rebukes his sword-wielding defender, but restores the severed ear of the victim, uttering stern words against such violence: "'No more of this!'" (Luke 22:51). Whether that restoration actually happened or not is not the question; the point is, What does it mean? Answer: It means Jesus' fervent dismissal of the whole paraphenalia of power, of winning by force, of conquering. Such conquering, like the severed ear, can only be destructive. Nobody is won over in that way, anyway. It only makes others more adamant in their determination to resist and repel. We shouldn't need two thousand years of "conquering for Christ" to convince us of that!

What I'm saying is that the allegedly "Christian" tendency to treat "the others" by trying to overpower them, whether with swords or only words, isn't Christian at all; it's just human, all too human. Moreover, according to Christian belief, one would have to say that it's part of what is radically wrong with our humanity. In fact, it's what Jesus came to change. It's part of a pent-up violence within us—a violence that usually, thank God, manages to limit itself to words and gestures, but is nevertheless violence. When Jesus told his disciples, "Love your enemies" (Matt. 5:44; Luke 6:27), he was countering that characteristic human violence in the most dramatic way. We think it is natural and excuseable to be violent with our enemies (I had my adolescence during World War II!), but even here, says Jesus, conquering has no business in the community of faith. I've said that the missionary dimension is just part of faith—Christians are "sent" people. But we're not sent out with swords, or even with powerful words, big claims, loud threats and promises, fabulous and flashy knowledge—maybe augmented by electronic music and strobe lights. Paul, certainly the most eloquent spokesperson of the earliest cohort of Christians, wrote to his little flock of converts in Corinth, "When I came to you, brothers and sisters, I did not come proclaiming the mystery of God to you in lofty words or wisdom. For I decided to know nothing among you except Jesus Christ, and him crucified. And I came to you in weakness and in fear and much trembling . . ." (1 Cor. 2:1-3). When Jesus nudged his apostles out of their comfortable, familiar "nest" into the world, the *oekumene*, he warned them, "I am sending you out as sheep into the midst of wolves" (Mark 10:16). The world is a violent place, but far from initiating worldly violence, the "missionary" Christians are counseled to submit to the violent and aggressive ones.

There can be no doubt in the mind of anyone who knows anything about Christian history that this very *human* impulse to "conquer" others was given a huge boost by the establishment of Christianity in the fourth century about which we've already been thinking. In fact, it's one of history's greatest ironies that the words the Emperor Constantine is supposed to have heard in his dream before the decisive battle of the Milvian Bridge were, *In hoc signo vinces*: "In this sign you will conquer." The sign he reputedly saw in his dream was the so called *chi-rho*, a symbol made up of the first two Greek letters of the title "Christos" (Christ).

Look: When you put together a strong human impulse (stronger than ever because it's pretty close to the essence of sin!) with a huge, military-based empire (one that's even more power-hungry than usual because it is visibly failing!), strange and terrible transformations can occur to a faith tradition, even one that contains a consistent criticism of power. And remember: Christianity has been bound up with one powerful (and often also threatened) empire after another, right down to our own "American Empire."

It is just not possible to overlook this political identity of Christendom when one thinks about the way that Christianity, historically speaking, has behaved toward other religions, as well as its own dissenters, deviants, and alleged heretics. Empires are governed by a built-in logic of power, even when they are relatively benevolent and enlightened empires such as we like to think (without so much justification!) the British and the American empires have been. And what empires want from their "established" religions, besides ritual and pageantry and the aura of the eternal, is the kind of "spiritual" backing that will reinforce their quest for power and their sense of destiny as superior societies. Christendom, so long as it was allied with empire—in other words, so long as it was Christendom!—has been obliged by its very association with imperial peoples to exclude and, sometimes, violently to seek to eliminate alternative religions, including of course the religions of the rival nations and empires, but also alternative religions cropping up within the precincts of Christendom itself.

Following this logic of empire, the habit of exclusion has been practiced in Christendom for a millennium-and-a-half. So it almost comes naturally to the remnants of Christendom still today to treat "the others" by excluding them. We don't put them to the sword or the stake today (or so we like to believe, so forgetful are we of the Holocaust), but there are subtle as well as obvious ways of excluding. When you hear fundamentalist Christians and others going on about there being "No Other Name," no way to salvation, no knowledge of God even, except through Jesus Christ, you should hear behind these claims centuries of Christendom's service to imperial Western peoples. Such Christians will of course find all kinds of scriptural justification for this position (what can't you find in the Bible when you're really looking for it?), but the real impetus behind this exclusivistic rhetoric is the long-standing association of Christianity with powerful empires, races, and classes of the Western world. This association is so firmly fixed that it is almost impossible for people to read newer Testamental statements like, "I am the Way, the Truth, and the Life" (John 14:6) without simply assuming that this means that "there is no salvation outside the church" (*Extra ecclesiam nulla salus*).

But suppose we take a statement like Jesus' "I am the way . . . ," which is attributed to Jesus by the writer of the Gospel of John; and suppose we even take it at its face value, assuming that Jesus really did say this (which may or may not have been the case). Let's even become more "literal" than the biblical literalists and listen to what John's Jesus actually says: "*I* am the Way, the Truth, and the Life". He does not say that this or that *doctrine* about him, or *image* of him, or *creed* concerning him, or *hymn* to him is "the Way," and so forth; he says that he himself ("I") is the way. Nor does he say that this means that only those who *say* that he is, indeed, the Way are going to be "saved." We've already heard about that—how saying "Lord, Lord" may get you nowhere (Matt. 25:31ff.).

So even on the basis of this biblical verse that is used so often by those who intend to exclude "the others," such a point can't be sustained. At the very least, faith must admit that the "I" of Jesus, his unique and inviolable Selfhood, cannot be captured by doctrines and dogmas and formulas and images and creeds. And must not faith go well beyond that and admit that "Yes, and this 'I' may be far more inclusive than we, his avowed followers, are!"? After all, the Jesus of the Gospels was always shocking his disciples by associating with people whom they considered outside the pale. Is it not likely that Christ's modern-day disciples are just as prone to restrict his associations to their own inner circle?

But let's consider yet another way of looking at all this (we've already touched on it before). If I ask myself as a Christian, "How has my faith in Jesus as God's representative affected my attitude toward others—other religions, other races, people of other sexual identity, and so forth?" then if I am being strictly honest with myself I must answer in some such way as this: I know that my own "natural" tendency, which has been reinforced by my familial, national, racial, class, and other background, is to look upon all or nearly all of these "others" with a kind of half-conscious suspicion, or at least a certain caution. I may have learned to hide or soften or sublimate that "gut" reaction, but I know all the same that it is deeply embedded in my psyche, part of my formation. The fact that I, by accident of birth, have belonged to a very "successful" race and a very powerful civilization only accentuates whatever "natural" tendency there may be in me to exclude others. But honesty compels me to admit that this tendency is still there in me, after all my humanistic education, and even after all my years of explicit Christian involvement.

What continues to counteract and transform this aboriginal exclusivity of mine is *chiefly* . . . Jesus Christ! Far from sanctioning or encouraging the "natural" habit of exclusion, the grace that comes from that Source constantly judges that habit, and strives to replace it with at least the beginnings of a far greater openness to others—greater, indeed, than I usually find comfortable! If I am not the chauvinist, the bigot, the sexist, the racist, and so on that I might otherwise have been (yes, I do not consider myself wholly superior to all that crowd!), it is *chiefly* because of the Nazarene. I cannot think of him—a person after all very different from myself, member of a completely different race, living in a quite different time, and so forth; I cannot think of him—a person astonishingly open to all sorts and conditions of human beings, mingling with the most despised people of his context, forgiving and blessing even his enemies, and finally laying down his life for people whom he could justifiably have ignored and written off: I simply cannot think of him, let alone remember that I regard him, in faith, as the very revealer of the *God* before whom my life is lived and judged; in short I cannot consider myself his follower and still give way to my own visceral feelings of suspicion or hesitancy or polite unconcern vis-à-vis "the others."

What am I saying here? I am saying that the gift—the *grace*—that makes faith possible in the first place is a grace that struggles against the many-sided spirit of alienation that is present in our spoiled, *self*-absorbed, *self*-preserving human "nature." I am saying that faith in *Jesus* as the one who makes God real and present to Christians, far from reinforcing and stimulating their sinful tendency to exclude others, positively drives them toward a greater—okay, a greater "inclusivity."

So yes: the preacher you heard on Sunday was right: Christians should be inclusive. I agree. But I also understand your hesitation about that sort of language, however well-meant it may be. It's very "in" language just now, along with a lot of other jargon. The language of inclusivity makes one important point, but it is largely a negative point: namely, *exclusivity* is un-Christian. But to describe the desirable alternative as *inclusivity* simply doesn't do justice to Christianity.

Inclusiveness may describe a certain attitude, an openness to difference, but it offers no explanation at all of why anybody would assume that attitude. The truth is, most of those who use this language don't think that any such explanation is needed, because their whole assumption is the "liberal" belief that the problem behind all this is just a moral one, or perhaps only a carryover from our unenlightened, monocultural past, and that with a little education exclusivists can learn how to become inclusivists. As I've implied above, I don't think the impulses behind the human tendency to exclude are that superficial. They reach down into our deepest insecurity, anxiety, and aboriginal estrangement. In conventional language, our all-too-human tendency to exclude "the others" is of the essence of what the Bible calls sin. It won't be changed easily! As I've implied in telling you those things about my own "natural" tendencies, that sin, too, like most of the others, persists even in those who know it to be profoundly countered by grace.

Even more importantly, what that grace wants to put in place of our excluding ways is not just the readiness to "include." "Including" also has its problems where "the others" are concerned. Too often, when we include others, besides just being plain condescending toward them, we are probably robbing these others of their own unique identities. I don't know about you, but I've often felt more resentful of "includers" than of those who openly exclude me. There's a very nice, liberal way of including one that is really just a matter of *ignoring* one—absorbing one's real otherness into some generalized and impersonal category called "different." If I'm going to be taken seriously by anybody, I don't want my difference from them to be overlooked or even minimized or generalized; I don't want to be just some little extension of their own egos, or some instance of the ideology they happen to be peddling. In fact, if they're going to pay any attention to me at all, I'd hope they would do me the favor of taking my otherness *more* seriously, not less.

Instead of using the liberal language of inclusivity to describe the Christian alternative to being exclusive, then, I would propose we adopt the *biblical* language of hospitality. There is probably no greater admonition to the people of Israel than the frequently repeated law of hospitality. Except when it was totally misunderstood, the Hebrew sense of being a "special" (elected or chosen) people never meant that being Jewish was by definition exclusive. Again and again, the prophets and lawgivers of Israel exhorted their people to exercise hospitality toward "the stranger." This was in fact a test of Israel's faith, for Jews knew always that they, too, had been "strangers in the land of Egypt," to mention only one of their many exiles, and strangers also to God.

This same theme is taken up in the newer Testament—for instance, by Paul, who writes, "Welcome one another [the older versions are even better, I think: "Receive one another"], just as Christ has welcomed you. For I tell you that Christ has become a servant of the circumcised on behalf of the truth of God in order that he might confirm the promises given to the patriarchs, and in order that the Gentiles might glorify God for his mercy" (Rom. 15:7-9).

Hospitality is not an empty, basically contentless idea like inclusiveness. It isn't just a bit of morality, a command; it has its basis in the very heart of the gospel. Listen to the progression of Paul's thought in what I just cited: You yourself have been received by Christ, therefore you have been given what it takes to receive others, therefore please do so!

Like all the key concepts of biblical faith (and unlike inclusivity!), hospitality is a *relational* concept. It honors the "otherness" of the others, because the important thing is really to relate to ("receive," "welcome") the others, not to absorb them into some supposedly neutral category, or (more likely!) into one's own ego or prearranged worldview. The biblical exhortation is not "Smother others," but "Welcome them." That means, among other things, "Let them be themselves! Don't try to overcome the distance between you and them by robbing them of their difference." That difference is the presupposition of your achieving a real relationship with them.

And why should anyone treat these others as if they were just candidates for conversion? Listen: the Jews and Muslims and

Buddhists and atheists and humanists and others with whom we rub shoulders on our public conveyances in every major city on this continent today have their own points of view, and most of them take their beliefs as seriously as Christians take theirs. No amount of conservative "exclusivity" is going to scare them into the church. Nor is any amount of liberal "inclusivity" going to dispel their commitment to their particular system of belief; it may even make them more resentful than the downright excluding Christians make them feel. The only people whose commitment is compromised or weakened in the liberal approach are the Christian inclusivists themselves, who have exchanged a serious faith commitment for a broadly humanitarian openness that begs the question of its own foundations. Liberal Christians think that by minimizing the uniqueness and centrality of Jesus Christ they can create a general sort of religiousness, a theism, or a theistic humanism, to which everyone would gladly give assent. Like the nineteenth-century Christian liberals who wanted to overcome the "scandal of particularity" we mentioned earlier, the new inclusivists are ready to downsize the role of Jesus in Christian belief so that "God," who seems (repeat: *seems*) more universal, can become the common rallying point for all believers. But, as we ought to know from the fate of nineteenth-century Christian liberalism, such an approach too easily ends up with nothing to offer—as we remarked earlier, no surprises, no challenges either. A "god" who is so general and all-encompassing as that; a "god" without a face, without features, without a voice; a "god" so nicely accessible to "enlightened" reason, so manipulable by human needs and trends—such a "god" never achieves sufficient Personhood or "Thou-ness," to be able to address us and engage us and struggle with us. Such a "god" only *reflects* us—namely, those of us who create this god in our own image of ourselves as enlightened people.

This is what I believe: instead of minimizing and generalizing and downplaying Jesus; instead of reducing him to a type or finding in him supposedly universal principles and ideas and moral teachings; instead of trying to overcome his particularity and so avoiding (or thinking to avoid) the scandal of it, let's go more deeply into his Person—deeply enough to discover *his* radical "otherness." If we are ready to open ourselves to the Other called Jesus, we shall discover (as I have) both the possibility and the necessity of hospitality toward all the others.

That approach, unlike both the exclusivists and the inclusivists, seems to me to meet the two "requirements" that you named when you said, insightfully enough, that while you don't want to be part of an "outfit" that by definition excludes three-quarters of humankind, neither could you take seriously a faith that asked for less than full and faithful commitment. My point is that genuine commitment to the triune God made concrete by Jesus and made present to us by the divine Spirit drives one to a far greater commitment to *the whole creation*, and especially all within it that is "other," than apart from faith would occur.

Is the new hospitality toward others that faith makes possible intended to serve the Christian mission by luring these others into the church? Is this hospitality, this "welcoming," a means to the end of world evangelism and conversion? Not to my mind. Such hospitality, worked out in all the concrete and particular ways that are demanded by the changing context, and imaginatively and faithfully lived by Christians, would itself and as such be a sufficient implementation of the Christian mission—at least for the present. What is more important: that the whole world should become nominally and reluctantly Christian, or that some portion of the world in every age should live and teach real hospitality toward others—a hospitality that loves and serves others, a stewardly hospitality, that does not have strings attached and does not offer itself only on the condition that the others acknowledge the Christian sources of this hospitality?

At least for the foreseeable future, the Christian mission to the world will have to be indirect and implicit, not direct and explicit. After sixteen-odd centuries of Christendom "conquering," few of the others, most of them victims of all that conquering, are going to find the verbal testimonies of Christians as such either persuasive or trustworthy. What is required now is the kind of earnest and informed commitment to Jesus as the Christ that will be prepared as he was, through self-sacrifice, voluntary suffering, and informed, disciplined service, to *be* Christians in the midst of the world. If that kind of Christianity is *lived*, there can be no doubt about it—some, perhaps many, will ask for "the reason why." Then, and I think only then, usually, will it be appropriate and good for Christians to speak openly about their faith and "the hope that is in them."

I know of course that those Christians who think it the calling of the disciples of Jesus Christ to try to make the whole world over into the church will not find my position at all to their liking. They will complain that I am capitulating to religious pluralism; that I am justifying the status quo; that I am allowing "the others" simply to go their own way, unquestioned, uninformed about salvation, and so forth. I know that nothing I say will convince my critics otherwise, but to *you* and others like you I will say that I do not accept their judgment. I am not a religious pluralist—I reject "plural*ism*" as I try to reject every other ideology, every *ism*. I am not justifying the present state of things—I am challenging the churches, for instance, to make radical changes in their behavior. Nor am I simply "allowing" the others to go their own way. They *will* go their own way, whether I "allow" it or not! What as a Christian I can and must allow is their right to be who they are, believe what they believe, practice their faith as they practice it. Given the grace and the law of love, and given also the way in which for centuries imperial Christendom thwarted that grace and disobeyed that law, I, who cast the long shadow of "Christendom" wherever I go, do not possess any "right" to correct other religions, whose adherents have in many cases exemplified that grace and that law far better than

Christians have! What I may and I think must do, whenever I am able to achieve some measure of trust on the basis of the new hospitality "in Christ," is to help those "others" discover within their own traditions the goodness, beauty, and truth that parallels, complements, and perhaps even purifies that of my own tradition; so that together, in a world that is both boringly secular and desperately yearning for transcendence, we can gradually discover that we have enough "in common" to be of some *worldly* use!

Is There Any Hope?

"This will have to be our last discussion—for now, at least," you said, after we'd exchanged the usual small talk; "I'm leaving for the summer as soon as my last exam has been written."

"Well, I'll miss these sessions," I responded. "They've been stimulating for me. I hope they have been useful to you as well, though I'm conscious of the fact that there are a great many subjects we've had to leave out. I hope you won't judge the whole Christian faith on the basis of the little time we've had to devote to it!"

"No, I won't—though I don't think you should be so apologetic about it. We have touched on some pretty central questions, it seems to me. I'm not quite as naive as I was. When I showed up in your study a few months ago I was pretty well convinced that Christianity could have no appeal for 'thinking people'—of whom, of course, I considered myself a rather striking example! I know now that I was wrong about that. I realize now how little I knew, and know—how much I still have to learn."

"And what do you plan to do about that?" I asked.

"Just now," you replied, "I am so tied up with the demands of my courses—well, and a lot of other things, too—that I haven't given much serious thought to any follow-through. At least, my ideas on the subject are still pretty vague. But one thing I have decided is that

I will begin this summer to read the Bible on a regular basis. Every-thing you have said about Christianity seems to presuppose some knowledge of that book. And by the way, I've been getting the same message from one of my English literature professors. She keeps call-ing it 'The Great Code'—says that nobody can understand Western literature without it."

"I imagine she learned that from a famous literary critic and pro-fessor at the University of Toronto, the late Northrop Frye. And it's quite right, too. But of course Christians consider biblical awareness necessary for more basic reasons than having a 'code' to other litera-ture, important as that is. In fact, most of the other literature in ques-tion (Milton, Blake, Melville, Tolstoy, Austen, Atwood—the lot!) refers to the Bible for the same reason Christians do: as an indispens-able source of truth and meaning."

"Are you saying that the Bible as such is true?" you asked.

"No, I'm not. Some would say that, but the Bible itself does not say that about itself. It always points beyond itself to a Truth it knows it can't contain. Remember the statement of Jesus we thought about earlier?— "I am the way, the truth, and the life. . . ." The words of the Bible are intended to bear witness to what the Bible itself calls God's Word. God's Word transcends all words. God's Word is a living, breathing, speaking voice—a voice that addresses us here and now, in all the ever-changing reality of our living. God's Word therefore, as the beginning of John's Gospel puts it, can only be incarnated in a life, a person, a 'thou.' For Christians, the words of the Bible point to the living Word that can't be reduced to words—the Word 'made flesh'—Jesus."

"So the Bible's actual words are not so important after all?"

"To the contrary! They're all the more important than if they were themselves to be regarded as the Truth, capital T. People who equate Truth with the Bible soon find themselves in trouble (though few of them admit it), because the Bible says many things, not all of which are consistent with one another. So what happens is that so-called biblical literalists pick and choose from these ancient texts what they themselves want to emphasize. And, since some choose this and others that, divisions quite naturally occur—and we end up with all these sects and churches, each claiming they've got hold of ultimate truth and hauling out their 'proof texts' to demonstrate it. What many of these people want to 'prove,' chiefly, is the absolute truth of their own beliefs. The Bible functions for them, not so much as an authority under which they stand, but as evidence of their own authority.

"For me (and I think it's my inheritance from classical Protestantism), the Bible is the Christian's guide—not in itself the Truth, but the chief written witness to Truth. I am beholden to it, as I would be to a witness to something about which I had no firsthand knowledge. If I come to understand it somewhat, I never feel that I have understood it fully; and I certainly don't consider it a ready endorsement of my own fondly held assumptions and beliefs. More often than not, the Bible challenges my ideas—makes me think again. Here, as I've said before, real 'understanding' means 'standing under.' The church is a community that 'stands under' the authority of the Scriptures—and can never put itself forward as though it were the Bible's possessor and sole interpreter. That's one reason why Christians should be glad that the largest portion of their Bible, the so-called Old Testament, is as much the Bible of Jews and, to some extent, Muslims, as well. We don't own it. In a real way, it owns us.

"So these biblical 'words' really are indispensable. They're indispensable in the first place because they are the words of unique witnesses; they're the only firsthand testimonies we have to the decisive events upon which Christian faith is founded.

"But more than that, the biblical traditions, whether Jewish or Christian, have an immense respect for words—for speech, for language, for the written and spoken word. God is a speaking God, and we are speaking creatures. Words in the age of advertising and among the chattering classes—including teachers like me—often seem cheap and facile. But they are still our primary mode of communication. There are a great many sayings in English that belittle speech—like Hamlet's 'Words, words, words,' or proverbs like 'Actions speak louder than words.' But when it comes right down to it, the most significant things we have to communicate to one another, including our deepest feelings as well as our most subtle ideas, absolutely require words. So you will not find these Hebrew-Christian Scriptures denouncing human words, except words that are patently flippant or purposely deceptive. All the same, the biblical writers knew that the truth they testified to could not be captured in the words they wrote, inspired as some of those words are.

"I always think Luther got it right when he said that the Bible is the 'cradle of Christ'—not the Christ, not what is ultimate; but nevertheless necessary as the vehicle through which the ultimate is communicated to us. He was right, too, when he said, 'The Bible has a wax nose!' It can easily be twisted to say what one wants to hear.

"But don't let me run on! You were saying that you want to begin reading the Bible seriously. That's good. But how will you do this? Will you need any help?"

"I thought," you replied, "that I could just—you know—pick it up, maybe just before bedtime, and read a chapter or so. Is that a bad idea?"

"No, you could likely profit from that if you did it thoughtfully. But I think you should have some help with interpretation, too. Remember, these are ancient texts, and even if you use a very modern translation you will encounter problems with the text. Or, what may be even worse, you'll too often think you understand when you don't. So at least you should look for a few books that will give you the necessary historical and linguistic background—I'll make a list for you, later."

"I suppose I could take a course next year—an elective. . . ."

"Yes, by all means do that, if you can work it in. But even if you can't, you can always look for a few other people who would like to become more familiar with 'the Great Code.' You might even ask whether such a group already exists in one of the churches you've visited—or, if it doesn't, ask the minister if you could help him or her get one going?"

"Maybe I will," you said—and I think you meant it. But it was obvious that your mind was already carrying you off in another direction. So I waited. It didn't take long.

"I'm thinking," you said, "that we've only got this hour or so, and there's something else I want to ask you about. Well, in fact there are a whole lot of things. As you said, we've had to leave out a good deal. But something—I suppose it's partly because the term is ending, and endings always stir things up in me—something has been bothering me all this week. As usual, it's rather hard for me to pinpoint the problem—it's not even a problem, I suppose, but an entire lifetime of problems! I don't even know where to begin."

"Just start anywhere," I suggested. "Talk around it. There are people who talk in order to tell themselves what they're thinking. Maybe you're one of them. I know I am."

"All right. . . . I watched a lot of television this week—even read some newspapers. The pressure of exams, you know. . . . It wasn't a great week in the life of the world, was it? Another huge oil spill. Another breakdown of peace talks in the Middle East. Continuing chaos in Albania. Starving refugees in Africa, hounded by civil war. Plans for the trial of the man accused of the Oklahoma City bombing. Inquiries into the conduct of peacekeeping forces, tainted blood, fraudulent mining claims . . . and so on.

"Oh, yes, and that group—'Heaven's Gate' I think they're called—whose religion induced them to take their own lives, thirty-nine of them, in the hope (according to them, the sure belief!) that they were going to be whisked off to some Paradise in the wake of that new comet. . . . They'd even packed their bags for the journey!

"I won't even mention all the personal disasters and tragedies the media reported—with a certain relish, as usual. And probably I needn't say anything, either, about the environment, or the economic situation of planet Earth, where 'the rich get rich and the poor get babies,' as an old song says.

"That's probably enough to set the stage for what I'm getting at. No, there's another thing—another whole dimension, I guess. Me! I'm a hopeless victim of hope. I've been brought up on the rhetoric of getting ahead, doing great deeds, progress. . . ."

"Not as unqualifiedly as my generation was, however," I interjected. "I grant you, the leftovers of what a friend of mine called the North

American religion, the Religion of Progress, are still around. Every TV ad drags them out and props them up—but then every news broadcast knocks them down again. Every person running for political office has to mouth them—but then few politicians actually behave as if they were true. There just isn't the kind of public credulity there used to be where progress is concerned. Few little boys today (and fewer little girls!) really believe they could become President of the U.S.A. or famous movie stars. Perhaps, given the no-longer-private lives of presidents and movie stars, few would even want that."

"Maybe so. But we're still encouraged to get an education, and then another education, and maybe another after that—diversify our skills, better our chances, become innovators, dream big globe-sized dreams, think success, and all that. And, besides, one has to keep trying, believing, hoping—it's almost biological! Even if one is cynical, like Ivan in The Brothers Karamazov, one feels the tug of life and the future in one's very stomach.

"But in the end, isn't that 'natural' drive to say 'Yes!' to life, to celebrate, to 'make something of your life' as you told me your grandmother had said to you when you were young—isn't all that just rather deceptive? False promises? Look at the external evidence, for heaven's sake—as detailed by the media for our daily entertainment! Look at the internal evidence, too. As Camus (I think it was) put it, 'Men die, and they are not happy.' Quite a summary of reality! Not the sort of thing you put on greeting cards, eh?"

"I think," I said (with a sigh, probably), "that I know where you're going. I've been there, too. Often."

"So how do you cope with it?" Do you just close your eyes and . . . believe? Put your hands over your ears so as not to hear all that 'world news'? Ring in Easter Sunday? More lilies to cover up the cross, please? . . . No, I guess you wouldn't do that. After what you've already told me you couldn't be that inconsistent. The truth is, I wouldn't even have asked you about all this if I thought you'd resort to that sort of thing.

"I mean, I've listened to you enough to know you couldn't just launch into joy and gladness in the face of my little outbursts of gloom. I even anticipated you'd say something sympathetic like, 'I've been there, too.' I believe that. But obviously you don't just accept being 'there.' You haven't concluded that 'there' is all there is—that death, so to speak, is the only live option. You wouldn't waste all this time with the likes of me if you had. So I want to ask you in all seriousness: Is there any hope? Hope for the world? For us? For me? Don't just tell me what your doctrine says—or even what the Bible says. I haven't forgotten our discussion of Paul on the subject of hope. But I want to hear what you *think*, how you *cope*."

"Is it so important what I say?"

"Yes. It is—to me it is. Now. It wouldn't have been eight or ten weeks ago when I walked into your room with my . . . my assumptions about all Christians. You remember, it was prior to Easter. The annual, predictable 'message of Easter' was already being given out. The stores, as usual, got it into the public mind long before the churches—just a tad after Christmas, in fact. But whether it came from the stores or the churches it seemed to amount to the same thing, basically: 'Don't believe the bad news, the good news is. . . . So lift up your hearts and take out your wallets.'

"Well, in the meantime you've convinced me that not all Christians have put on blinders—or (what was it Marx said?) 'taken dope.' I know you won't answer my question about hope by offering me an Easter egg. On the other hand, I still don't know how *you* will answer it. Sometimes, listening to you or reading what you wrote, I thought to myself, 'Maybe he's more like me than I thought. Maybe he's 'on the edge' of faith, too—as he said of me a couple of times. . . .'

I had to sit there for a minute or so, trying to take in what you were saying about me. My first reaction was to be a little miffed. Why should you consign me to the edges?—a Christian professional, a professor of Christian theology, an ordained minister of the church? Wasn't it enough that I had given my whole life to this faith? What more could you ask. . . ?

Then I realized the generosity of the affirmation I had just been handed. Some of my own words to you came back, like accusing echoes: "What use is a friend who stands above you and offers his sympathy?" "*The church has to participate in human disbelief and doubt to be at all credible to the world of disbelief and doubt.*" *Doubt and disbelief, like those other Ds, death and the demonic, are not visitors one welcomes. One would like to be free of them altogether! One would like to say yes to everything, accept everything, and (especially if one is a professor!) know everything. But what sort of "ambassador for Christ" would one be if that were the case? Just another of Job's friends, offering one's enlightened observations from a safe distance. "No problem!"*

I had emphasized several times that faith is not sight, the journey is not the arrival; and you had taken me at my word. I might be a little farther on in my journey than you are, but at least it seemed to you the same journey we were taking. We were participants in the same struggle, searchers after the same peace that "passes [without despising!] understanding," hungering and thirsting for the same truth and goodness. If my continuing doubt and lingering disbelief made it possible for people like the two of us, so far apart in so many ways, to meet, and talk, and learn how to care about one another, that was justification enough for the presence of those unwelcome visitors, Doubt and Company!

By the same token, this new recognition of the extent of your trust was accompanied by the realization I would have to work hard if I were going to respond to your question as sincerely as you had asked it. Without knowing it, you had just given me one of the most demanding assignments of my career.

The results, such as they are, are being sent to you at the summer address you left with me. Bon Voyage!

Be Strong, Take Courage!

I haven't done this before in my little essays for you, but this time I will give you a text—a couple of verses of Scripture on which to center your thought. Probably it will sound more like a sermon than an essay. I only hope you won't consider it a "pep talk"—

remembering as I do your dislike of the same! I know you want to hear my own response to your "lifetime of questions," but I think I can express myself best if I weave my thoughts around a text that I like very much. If you remember nothing else from this statement of mine, you may at least remember these lines of the psalmist:

> I believe that I shall see the goodness of the Lord
>   in the land of the living.
> Wait for the Lord;
>   be strong, and let your heart take courage;
>   wait for the Lord! (Ps. 27:13-14)

These words would be hollow and predictable if they were uttered by someone who didn't know how hard it is to do the very things the words ask of us. It's easy to "believe" if you have never been assailed by radical unbelief, and to "wait" if you think you already have everything you need; and it's easy to be "strong"—or seem so—if you have had no occasion to discover your actual weakness, or "courageous" if you've never had to face any great crises in your life. But these words, which are the last lines of Psalm 27, become interesting and credible when one considers the clues about the life of the writer as they are implied in the twelve verses of the Psalm that *precede* this "final word."

Those twelve verses show us a person who knows fear and cowardice, feels surrounded by "adversaries" (is there a little paranoia here?), is acquainted with war and injustice and the betrayal of even close friends and family members; a person, moreover, who understands that his or her "trouble" is not due only to the bad will of others, or an impersonal fate, but is the consequence, in part, of personal shortcomings—which is why the writer senses that God might indeed "turn away in anger," "cast me off," "forsake me." In short, because this psalm grows out of the experience of some of life's real negations, its positive conclusion does not sound hollow or merely rhetorical.

And there is another point, even more important: the last lines I've quoted above are in the imperative mood: "Wait for the Lord;

be strong, and let your heart take courage; wait for the Lord!" All commands—Do this! Now, if these commands were all that we had, we would be justified in thinking, "Fine! Great advice! Just what I want! But, unfortunately, I can't come up with that kind of courage and strength, and I'm sick of waiting."

But if you read the rest of the psalm, you'll see that this exhortation to be strong, have courage, and patiently wait presupposes another experience: the experience of God's faithfulness—

> The Lord is my light and my salvation;
>   whom shall I fear?
> The Lord is the stronghold of my life;
>   of whom shall I be afraid? . . .
> [Even] If my father and mother forsake me,
>   the Lord will take me up. . . .

. . . and so (the next-to-last verse): "I believe that I shall see the goodness of the Lord in the land of the living."

In other words, we are not asked to manufacture strength, invent courage, concoct hope out of thin air, improvise a whole new outlook on life. This is not a self-help course, or ten steps toward positive living. It's grace. It's gospel. God is already "there" for you—*is* your "light and salvation," *is* the "stronghold of your life," is committed to you and will not "forsake" you.

This is the presupposition of everything else. This is the only thing, really, that you are asked to believe. All the rest is just to help you with that—with trust. And even with that you aren't asked to do it all on your own. Trust in God doesn't occur as the result of a command; it's a response to something given—grace. You'll know very well (the more familiar you become with the life of the faith, the better you'll know it) that this trust isn't something *you* come up with, all by yourself. And you will also know—I think you already do know this, in a way—that God is "with you" and "for you" even when you don't believe, or think you don't believe, or only half-believe—or even when, standing on the edge of faith, you've begun to feel that such belief would be desirable. Believe me, *God does not depend on our belief in God.* Even if our faith were unchallenged by any doubt; even (to speak foolishly) if it were one hundred percent trust (which in fact it never is), it would only represent a very tiny fraction of the grace that makes it possible in the first place. It's that grace that matters most, not our appropriation of it.

This has to be where hope begins, this is the foundation: God's "prevenient" grace—the grace that goes before us, anticipating already what our real needs will be. Speaking out of this *fundamental*—this foundation—the psalmist is enabled, despite all the fearful things by which he or she is surrounded, to affirm: "I believe that I shall see the goodness of the Lord in the land of the living."

With that as *our* basis, too, let's consider your question: Is there any hope? You want to know *my* answer. You want me to speak personally, as one human being on the edge of faith to another. Very well, I shall. First, let me take on the big question—at least, it's the one you started with: whether there's any hope for "us," our civilization, our world. After that, I'll say a little about the individual side of this—about "Me."

It's interesting how the psalmist expresses the nature of historical hope: *"I believe that I shall see the goodness of the Lord in the land of the living."*

You know, in one respect that's a very bold claim; but in another respect it's wonderfully modest. It's bold because it doesn't reserve the object of hope for "later"—pie in the sky by and by. I expect to see God's goodness "in the land of the living"—already now! And it's also bold because the author, as we saw, is not naive about evil. There's a courageous kind of "nevertheless" involved here: "In spite of all this wickedness, these bad things that happen to good people, this moral ambiguity of the otherwise good people themselves, and so forth, *nevertheless* I believe that I'll see God's goodness here and now."

When you raised this question, you began by presenting a rather devastating thumbnail sketch of all the terrible things happening in our world just now. Well, there *are* terrible things, and Christians, like other people of integrity, should not ignore them. It is also true that we are living in a rather bleak period—a period when a great many dreams have failed, when crass entrepreneurial aggressiveness seems impervious to the cries of the poor and marginalized, and so on. But two points have to be made about all this, from the Christian perspective as I understand it:

First, our awareness of the world we live in should not be formed too one-sidedly by the more dramatic events of the moment—and especially not by what is reported by the popular media. Many wise observers of our society have spoken and written about the inordinate influence of television, especially. TV "news" functions, not only as an almost exclusive source of world information for the majority of North Americans, but it functions (you said this yourself) as "entertainment." Networks are in fierce competition with other networks, and what sells best as entertainment is sex, scandal, violence, fraud—the whole Pandora's box of human wretchedness. That in itself, of course, says a good deal about who we are as a people—alas! Is it to be attributed to our boredom? Is there some sort of death-wish in our fascination with such "news"? Or is it just that it makes us feel safe and cozy on our couches, munching our potato chips, when we can watch others suffer—is it the ultimate sort of distancing from pain and trouble?

Whatever the reason, my point just now is to say: It's not all true, it's not an accurate mirror of reality. When did you last hear a news broadcast that grew excited over the fact that several hundreds of healthy babies had been born in the city that day, and several hundreds of lives had been saved by (untainted!) blood donated by people who cared, and thousands of children had eaten relatively healthy meals, and so on? If one child had been brought into a police station badly bruised, obviously abused; if one kindergarten attendant had through neglect caused a serious accident; if one husband had gone berserk and shot his family—you can be sure you'd hear about it. *That's* news! But it isn't the whole story by a long shot.

The trouble is, given the enormous social influence of what Marshall McLuhan called the "hot" media, attitudes are created that in the end lead to a very fatalized conception of reality. For instance, in some urban parts of this continent people are so convinced that thieves are just waiting for them to leave their houses and apartments that many don't leave, while most others have become so security-conscious that they spend thousands of dollars on allegedly preventive equipment and personnel—much to the delight of certain manufacturers and agencies! We all know by now that nobody should *ever* walk on the streets of New York City, especially at night—and I have the impression that North Americans don't walk in *any* of their cities any more, night *or* day! We could go on in this vein.

Over against all this, the psalmist says (and so do I!): "I expect to see the goodness of the Lord in the land of the living." And both the psalmist and I insist on this *though we are not constitutional optimists!* It's just a matter of trust—trust in *God,* and therefore also of a certain *mistrust* of most other sources of truth about reality, especially those that are so uncritically believed by the majority. There will be something wrong with the world so long as human beings are sinners and we are all living under the conditions of history; but the wrong will never exist unchallenged, because the world God made is "good," is "loved," and will not be abandoned. Good and evil will strive for supremacy—and they will always be strangely mixed up with each other. But "I expect to see the goodness of the Lord in the land of the living"—and even the evil, which may sometimes seem to obliterate that goodness altogether, often mysteriously leads to a goodness that it could neither produce *nor* prevent. For the God who submits to the very source and core of evil, the God of Golgotha, is able still to make "even the wrath of men to praise him" (Ps. 76:10).

The second point that Christian realists (such as I try to be) have to make in relation to the kind of fatalization that has gripped so many people in our society is this: Human beings are not mere spectators! When the psalmist writes that he or she "expects to *see* the goodness of God in the land of the living" the intention is not to say: "I'm just going to sit here at my window—or in front of my TV screen—and watch for evidences of God's goodness"; rather, genuinely to be caught up in such "expectation" (that is, hope) means to become a participant in the "goodness" God is laboring to realize "in the land of the living." That is the reason why the psalmist ends with this call to strength and courage. It's also the reason why Jesus called disciples to *follow* him. Discipleship isn't just a matter of believing certain things, or being pious; it has to do with following the One who beckons us. He wants to take us—as he took Peter and the original disciples—into the very heart of this world's darkness, where the light we've been given, however dimly it may shine in us personally, can make some difference. (Have you ever noticed how far even something as simple as a smile or a kind word goes in our impersonal, fast, urban life?)

Listen: History, as Christians understand it, is not fixed, settled, set down according to some eternal game plan. Some things can be changed, and by us, individually and corporately. I don't mean that we "make history"—that's a grand modern illusion; but we are nevertheless part of history's making. There doesn't *have* to be so much poverty, illiteracy, race-prejudice. Gender wars and culture wars are not built into the very scheme of things. It is not written in stone that thirty-five million American citizens shall have no medical insurance at all. We are all going to die, but it's not a foregone conclusion that so many of us have to die as a result of AIDS, or motor accidents, or the pollution of the atmosphere, and so on. Nature will have its revenges on us if we continue to abuse it as we do; but we don't have to abuse it—not *that* much!

So "Be strong, take courage." God is on the side of life; and we, who (it's true) are often strangely attracted to death, may nevertheless be raised to life—enticed away from death—by the God who brought Jesus from the dead. By grace, we can learn, not only how to recognize the goodness of God in the land of the living, but how to participate in it ourselves—how to be stewards of that mysterious, transforming goodness.

Yes, this is a bold statement. But I said it is also a modest one. Why?

Well, think of what the psalmist *could* have said. He might have written, "I expect to see the inauguration of the classless society." Or "I expect to experience the end of all pain and suffering, the overcoming of all hostilities between people and nations, the realization of universal peace." Or "I expect to witness the final triumph of technology over all the limitations of knowledge and threats of nature—over death itself!"

He might even have said (many nineteenth-century liberal Christians did!), "I expect to see the kingdom of God in our time."

Ah! Now what are we going to do with *that*? We're on dangerous ground here! Because, as we already saw, the "kingdom of God" (which many of us now would rather call the "reign of God" or "realm of God," to avoid unnecessary sexist language)—seems to be a very basic Christian teaching. According to most biblical scholars, it is the central theme of Jesus' own teaching and the object of his work as the "Christ" or "Messiah." He begins his ministry in Galilee with the following announcement, according to Mark's account: "The time is fulfilled, and the kingdom of God has come near; repent, and believe in the good news" (Mark 1:15).

Fired by such a thought, Christian groups throughout the ages have imagined themselves citizens of God's already-achieved kingdom, or they have excitedly announced the dates of its fulfilment, with the return of the glorious Christ as king. The year 2000, the beginning of a new millennium according to the Christian calendar, is particularly attractive to such a mentality. Some of the best-selling religious books of our own period have been devoted to the subject—often enough with the implication that the advent of the kingdom must mean the destruction of this world. All over this continent, signs and billboards and graffiti announce the imminent return of the triumphant Christ, the judgment of this world, and the establishment of God's righteous kingdom—for a very select "raptured" minority.

The psalmist did not expect that sort of thing. And neither do I. And neither—*I* would say—did Jesus! What Jesus announced was the reality of God's reign. In this he was completely in line with the prophets of the older Testament and that strange figure in the newer Testament, his cousin John the Baptizer, whom the Gospel writers present as a representative of the whole prophetic tradition of Israel. Judaism, in both its biblical and postbiblical expressions, is a remarkably *expectant* faith. If you consider the history of the Jewish people, you are struck repeatedly by the thought: How amazing, that a people subjected to so much suffering should be so exceptionally committed to this world—to life (remember the Jewish toast, *L'chaim!*—To life!). Jesus was a Jew, also in this. One may say, to be sure, that he was *more* expectant, or more *consistently* expectant, than many authors of older Testament books— for example Lamentations, or Ecclesiastes, or perhaps even Amos and Jeremiah. But I think one cannot legitimately claim that Jesus represents a complete break with Judaism in terms of what he hopes for.

He is neither utopian nor wildly apocalyptic. In my opinion, he would have agreed with neither the utopianism of those nineteenth-century liberal Christians who expected the twentieth century to witness the ultimate achievement of divine love and justice on earth, nor the apocalyptic theories of the Christian dwellers on the Book of Revelation who seem to gloat over the destruction of planet Earth as much as they do over the "rapturing" of the elect into the heavenly kingdom. The latter is a particularly questionable view (I am tempted to say it is downright obnoxious!), because no faith that is as committed to creation as is this Judeo-Christian tradition could regard the destruction of this world as something hopeful! The liberal Christians were at least not guilty of that sin. Their error was in confusing the general optimism and euphoria of nineteenth- and early twentieth-century Western progressivism with Christian hope. They didn't grasp the subtle nuances of the biblical testimony to God's reign.

By that I mean the mystery of the divine "kingdom." It's there, for instance, in many of the parables of Jesus—for instance, the "Parable of the Growing Seed":

> [Jesus] also said, "The kingdom of God is as if someone would scatter seed on the ground, and would sleep and rise night and day, and the seed would sprout and grow, he does not know how. The earth produces of itself, first the stalk, then the head, then the full grain in the head. But when the grain is ripe, at once he goes in with his sickle, because the harvest has come." (Mark 4:26-29)

The seed has been planted, and it is a good seed. It is also a very small seed, as Jesus will say in the parable that follows—that of the "Mustard Seed," "the smallest of all the seeds on earth" (Mark 4:30-32). It has been planted, it is growing, it will mature and bear fruit; and, small as it is, the seed will produce something quite splendid—like a shrub in which the birds can nest!

You see, he is not talking about something big and impressive and, above all, *obvious*. And this is entirely consistent with the other metaphors he uses: a bit of yeast that makes the dough rise, a little salt to savor otherwise insipid food, a little light in the darkness, a little city on a hill lighted with oil lamps guiding the wandering stranger in the dark night. God's sovereignty, seen from the perspective of ordinary sight, is a small affair—for the most part, not even vaguely discernible! God's reign is completely unlike that of Caesar, or Louis XIV, or Elizabeth the First. There is little pomp and circumstance, little glory. No Händelian fireworks music! It's more like Bach. The glory there is, is a strange, unheard-of glory—the glory of a love that gives itself for the beloved. "O sacred Head, now wounded. . . ." God reigns from the cross. Only faith can see the effects of such a reign.

But faith *does* see them—at least here and there, now and then. Let's not exaggerate the matter! Faith is faith, not sight—as we've had to remind ourselves several times before. Anyway, faith *as such* is not what counts here. What matters is the seed, the yeast, the salt, the candle, the little city on the hill.[1] The seed is growing, the yeast is leavening, the salt is savoring, the candle is lighting up a lot of darkness, the little city is giving direction to the stranger wandering about on the hill in the night.

Certainly the growth of the seed (to stick with that metaphor) is not unhindered. There are weeds vying with it for sun and space. Besides, the earth in which it has been planted—the poor earth of humanity's soul—is not very conducive to its growth. All the same, the seed is growing. And faith trusts that it will continue to grow and, eventually, produce grain, and become ready for harvesting. Here and there it seems, sometimes, that the fields are already ripe for harvest (John 4:35)!

Do you see what I mean? It's a modest vision. It doesn't rush into utopian ecstasy over what is just around the corner, and it certainly doesn't long for the end of the world—only for the end of the world's "groaning" (Rom. 8:22). I know that Bible verses can be found to challenge my interpretation (the Bible is a happy hunting ground for every sort of *ism*, positive or negative!); but I am trying to remain true to the main thrust of biblical thought about hope and history. And that, I believe, is very succinctly expressed in the psalmist's sentence: "I believe that I shall see the goodness of the Lord in the land of the living." Jesus, I believe, could have said that without altering a word. He likely did, in his own language, and not just once.

The "reign of God" is the Christian faith's way of speaking concretely about that kind of expectancy. It is not an abstract conception of "what might be"; it is a concrete vision of "what is coming to be." It is not an ideal that always and forever must transcend the real world, nor is it, on the other hand, an exact program of action for us to implement. It is a statement about the justice, peace, truth, and love that are the essence of God's "goodness." "God is at work in the world to make and to keep human life human," as a great American theologian, Paul Lehmann, put it.[2] We, through faith, believe that we can see this now and then, here and there. More than that, we know ourselves to be invited and commanded and enabled to participate in it.

Christian theology does not offer a blueprint for the future. There is no five-year-plan, nor five-hundred-year plan either! Faith knows enough about what the *goal* is, however—I mean, God's goal—to allow human beings of "good will" wherever they be—in the church or out of it, faithful or on the edges of faith—the freedom they need to make decisions, take risks, make mistakes, try again . . . and again . . . and again. We may fail. Whole nations and civilizations may disappear—many have already. Churches too will come and go, as they always have done. What remains, as Luther wrote at the end of his famous hymn, following Augustine, the patron of his order: "the city of God."

I should probably end this there, as Luther did. But I'm thinking about your "Me"—what about me? You are right to insist on that. No affirmation of Christian hope is complete if it stops with the world at large, creation, the cosmos! I suppose that sounds a little ridiculous, really. After all, the fate of the earth, of the cosmos (!), is a subject far greater than . . . me. How infinitely small one seems in the perspective of the galaxies! Geological time always unnerves me utterly. How could I imagine—what arrogance!—that my life matters in the least, seen over against the backdrop of all that. I can't even envisage the figures, the mathematics. What is a billion, really? One thing for certain: it's a lot more than one.

And yet . . . this "one" is the only entree I have into that immensity. And that applies to all the other "ones," too. A lot of us may get together and become "we." We may form research teams and think tanks and universities and study the great wide world; and we are inevitably units within communities, societies, nations, civilizations, and so on. But each one of us lives in a body that, try as we might, can't meld with other bodies; each one of us has a face—a unique visage. In our lonely tower we look out through little "peepholes" (that's what Kurt Vonnegut calls eyes in one of his novels) onto a scene that always, no matter how familiar it may become, or how friendly even, is still . . . "out there."

And do we dare imagine ourselves, these tiny me's, *included* in the "land of the living" in which we expect to "see the goodness of God" at work, world without end?

I entered my seventieth year not long ago—the biblical age, as they say. As I think I mentioned to you before, I am in a position now that I did not occupy at age twenty-one: that is, I can say with a certain real confidence, I *have* seen the goodness of the Lord in the land of the living—and quite specifically in my own life, which, being pretty favored on the whole, does not require an enormous effort of faith to produce such a conclusion.

But my retrospective vision is in that respect more certain than my prospective outlook. I am well aware by now that these eyes will close, this face dissolve, this speech end. I lie awake sometimes trying to imagine what it must be like not to be. Usually I get up early on those nights, hoping to extend a little my being—with the result, alas, that I just reduce the quality of being for the rest of that day ("Who, by taking thought, can add one cubit to his span of life?" Matt. 6:27).

What I am trying to tell you is that I have no illusions about the mortality of the so-called Homo sapiens. "All flesh is grass" (Isa. 40:6; 1 Peter 1:24). I listened to a beautiful choral work of Brahms last night: "Even beauty must die." Even Mozart had to die—and so young! Rembrandt, like me, enjoyed a longer life, *Deo gratia.* But read his thoughts in his many self-portraits. Even such great art must come to an end. And it is not otherwise for us "lesser lights." Even this wonderful (if rather small and problematic!) body I live in and *am*; even these (now somewhat arthritic) hands that love to play the piano and write little yellow words on a computer screen; even this mind (average in most respects) that is a little kingdom of its own, full of unique memories and strange stirrings and unbidden thoughts—all of this that is "me" (I will not even speak of the other me's I love, it is too painful!) must come to an end, and sooner rather than later, now.

Well, and what then?

I have no idea. Christians, contrary to the opinion of some of them (!), do not believe in immortality—as if we *couldn't* die, really; and neither do they have a road map of the afterlife. Medieval and other forms of Christian pious imagination, usually well-stocked with pagan mythology, produced an enormous and detailed catalog of the accoutrements of heaven and hell, limbo, purgatory, and what-have-you. But the Bible, that (let me say it once more) *sane* collection of writings, is amazingly modest in its claims to all such knowledge. To be sure, its images and metaphors have been and continue to be turned into "facts" by the literalizing mind of the aforementioned Homo sapiens. But in itself—and given the fact that its prescientific context *could* have allowed a freer rein to the imagination—the Bible is remarkably reserved in its discussion of what lies beyond our earthly existence. It seems content to leave heaven to God.

It confesses—note well, *confesses!*—the resurrection of the dead.

This is the point where we know (though we should have known it all along) that everything depends on grace. Resurrection can neither be demonstrated rationally, nor experientially (the resuscitation of persons clinically dead notwithstanding); nor can we find the "wherewithal" for it in ourselves. That is how it differs from immortality. Immortality implies that the stuff of deathlessness lies in ourselves—in our "immortal souls." The biblical view of human being assumes an inviolable connection between spirit and body— a connection that religion, including the Christian religion, has regularly violated! Resurrection is the ultimate declaration of God's grace. It is not . . . natural. It is not . . . automatic. It is wholly dependent upon the faithfulness, forbearance, and love of God.

And just for that reason—only that!—I am able, usually, to sleep at night, to continue playing the piano and writing yellow words and taking my aging body more or less for granted "in the meantime." Because the only thing of which I can be at all confident when I think of my own "not being" is that God will be, I am not so presumptuous as to think that the God who "brought again our Lord Jesus Christ from the dead" (Heb. 13:20) will also, quite naturally, be pleased to bring me from the dead, too. I don't understand all that. . . .

Forgive me if I play this word game with you just once more, but it is quite literally true: I do not, and I expect I never shall, *understand* all that. All that I can do is to *stand under it.* Often, for instance, I stand gazing up at this great affirmation of Paul's—

> For I am persuaded, that neither death, nor life, nor angels, nor principalities, nor things present, nor things to come, nor height, not depth, nor any other creature, shall be able to separate us from the love of God, which is in Christ Jesus our Lord. (Rom. 8:38-39)

There is no way of *fathoming* that affirmation, or dissecting it, or analyzing its parts in such a way that they add up to its grand summation. Here understanding is surpassed. Here reason, whose needs and possibilities we have honored throughout these discourses of ours, can only bow its head and listen.

Listen . . . and wait.

So let me make these words of the ancient psalmist my final words to you, my dear friend and fellow traveler—

> Wait for the Lord;
>   be strong, and let your heart take courage;
> wait for the Lord.

Afterword

I conceived this book as an exercise in what is conventionally called Christian apologetics. Apologetic theology is theology that wants to make contact with the ordinary life and thought of people in a given sociohistorical context, one's own. Like the Christian apologists of the second century C.E., this exercise in apologetics aims to clear away misunderstandings of Christian faith current in its context, and establish points of common concern between the Christian message and the human situation.

It is my impression (as the discerning reader will have gathered) that the *greatest* misunderstandings of Christianity present in our American and Canadian context today are misundertandings perpetrated and perpetuated by Christian bodies themselves. The ancient, pre-Constantinian apologists had to contend with erroneous conceptions of the faith originating in pagan hearsay and rumor; today's apologists have to deal with simplistic, one-sided, and misleading representations of Christian belief and practice stemming from avowedly *Christian* sources.

Among the latter, ultraconservative, biblicist, fundamentalist, and doctrinaire Christianity is probably the most damaging; because this kind of "true belief" has all but captured the media; and the media, especially television, are today almost custom-made for the most unsophisticated, unnuanced, sloganized, and crassly "entertaining" versions of Christian belief. I do not regard Christian ultra-conservativism as in itself dangerous or even deeply offensive. As a wise Christian acquaintance used to say, "There are worse forms of darkness." But when, through the medium of modern communications technology and the aggressiveness of the marketeers, such phenomena as "the Christian Right" are able almost to achieve a monopoly hold on the very *meaning* of Christianity, it is necessary for serious Christian apologists to resist it and offer a more thoughtful—even if less "entertaining"—alternative.

If, then, I have addressed myself frequently, in this book, to misunderstandings arising from that source, it is because for so many of our contemporaries *that* has become normative Christianity; and my construction worker correspondent is quite right in finding such Christianity unacceptable "for anyone who 'thinks' to any significant degree" (see the Preface). And if, in my attempt to combat that religious simplism, I have quoted the Bible more frequently than any other document, it is because I am not ready to let that immense treasure house of spiritual wisdom become the sole property of the biblicistic simplifiers.

There is also another source of concern that serious Christian apologists today have to consider. It is the kind of Christianity that is so keen to be *au courant* that it ends by reflecting rather than engaging its culture. What worries me about some liberal forms of Christianity, including some that detest the adjective "liberal" and like to be thought "radical," is that it is so out of touch with the Christian tradition—and often, in fact, deliberately so—that in the last analysis it has nothing to say to our very confused and chaotic culture that is not already part of the Babel chatter. Too much liberal Christianity, including a good deal of what passes for high Christian scholarship, seems ready to let the Scriptures go, along with the classical, medieval, and reformation traditions of theological thought. If Christianity allows itself to forget its own traditions of wisdom, it will have little relevance to a society drowning in mere "information," while suffering profoundly from "cultural amnesia."[1] Traditional*ism* is as much the enemy of faith as any other "ism." But unless the churches (particularly the once-mainline Protestant denominations) can learn again how to recollect and struggle with what has been "handed over" [*tradere*] to them from the past, they will surely disappear from the cultural horizon even more quickly than their present statistics suggest.

An apologetic theology does not attempt to say everything. It is governed by the desire to *respond*—to "connect" with the questions that it senses are present, explicitly or implicitly, in its here-and-now. I have no wish to pretend, therefore, that all the great doctrines, dogmas, and intellectual concerns of the Christian faith have been addressed in this present work. There are in fact many omissions, and many subjects have been more hinted at than treated.

Anyone who has attempted Christian apologetics, however, will realize that for every "hint," every passing reference, there must be a great deal of hidden forethought—often years in the formation. Those who are troubled by omissions in this work, therefore, or who for any reason want to know more about what its author thinks concerning any aspect or dimension of this faith tradition, are requested to consult my other works, especially my major systematic theological study—the trilogy subtitled *Christian Theology in a North American Context*.[2]

I am grateful to the eighteen clergy of various Christian denominations who heard and responded to the first public airing of these chapters in May 1997, at the Toronto School of Theology;

and to the persons who heard them, and gave me some very useful "feedback," at the Montreat Conference Center of the Presbyterian Church, U.S.A., in North Carolina in July of the same year. I am particularly grateful also to my son, who read the manuscript in its initial form, and gave it the benefit of his "faithful doubt'—or perhaps doubtful faith! And, as always, I am grateful to Rhoda.

Notes

Chapter 1. Why Christian?

1. For example, Alasdair MacIntyre, in *Difficulties in Christian Belief* (London: SCM Press, 1959), 97ff.

Chapter 2. Why Jesus?

1. The expression originated with Louis XII of France (1462–1515), who said of his prime minister, Cardinal Georges d'Amboise, an ambitious and powerful politician, *Laissez faire à Georges, il est homme d'age* (Let George do it, he's the man of the hour). The saying was popularized by George McManners, an American cartoonist, who in the early 1900s created a series of cartoons based on the idea of shirking one's responsibility and leaving important decisions and actions to somebody else.

2. "Christ" is a title, not Jesus' surname! It is the English form of the Greek word *Christos*. *Christos* was the word chosen by translators of the Hebrew Bible into Greek to convey the Hebrew word that we anglicize as "Messiah." Both the Greek and the Hebrew terms connote the idea of "the anointed" or "the chosen" one. Kings and high priests in ancient Israel were anointed with oil to signify their being divinely chosen for these offices. "Messiah," however, came to be associated with the hope of Israel's liberation, and messianic expectation and longing were prominent in the period prior to and during the life of Jesus—due in part, of course, to Israel's oppression by Rome.

3. Reputedly the last words of the German poet Heinrich Heine (1797–1856).

4. This is one of the ways in which scholars translate the most important Hebrew word for God, *Yahweh.*

Chapter 3. Saved from What? For What?

1. In the fourteenth century, bubonic plague decimated Europe, carrying off at least one-third and possibly as much as one-half of the population.

2. See Tillich's *The Courage to Be* (New Haven and London: Yale University Press, 1952).

3. *Markings,* trans. Leif Sjöberg and W. H. Auden (New York: Alfred A. Knopf, 1965), 86.

4. It would be a good idea at this point just to pause and read through the Gospel accounts of Jesus in their entirety. It could easily be done in an afternoon.

5. A great American preacher, George Buttrick, used to tell his students in precisely those words that *that* must be the underlying message conveyed in every sermon.

6. See, for example, Matt. 9:21-22; 14:36; Mark 5:28; 6:56; 10:52; Luke 8:48-50; 17:19. (The newer translations often use the verb "to heal" where the King James and older versions employ the language of "wholeness"; but the linguistic origins of "heal" [hence also "health"], as can be readily observed in the adjective "hale," are the same as those of wholeness.)

Chapter 5. What's the Difference?

1. I am basing this example on an actual experiment carried out by a professor of communications in California. He asked his class of approximately one hundred students to write one page in response to the question, "How do you think the computer will affect your future?" With the exception of one or two responses, *all* were expressive of negative thoughts in response to the question. Next day, the professor announced he would read excerpts from all the responses, and he asked whether his students would permit him to divulge the names of the respondents as he read. Overwhelmingly they answered "No." Then, as he read the responses aloud, he observed growing astonishment in the class. They

had voted against his divulging their names because *each one feared he or she was alone* in thinking such bleak thoughts, *and* that to have this known would be to jeopardize even further their chances of success. In short, a climate has been developing in which it seems unacceptable to be critical of this complex technology. One may be truthful about all manner of things—sexual identity and preference included, but for one's own survival in a highly competitive "knowledge-world," one must keep one's feelings about this technology to oneself. (Source: CBC Radio "Ideas," Broadcast of Monday, February 24, 1997.)

2. The Apostles' Creed, which contrary to its name and early reputation did not originate with the twelve apostles but grew out of an old Roman statement of faith and is used only in Western churches; and the Nicene Creed, which is more elaborate than the Apostles' Creed, and is based on decisions made at the important early councils of Nicaea (325 C.E.) and Constantinople (381 C.E.). The Nicene Creed is the only *universally* used (ecumenical) creed of Christians.

3. From the opening lines of a contemporary Christian creed used in the United Church of Canada: "We are not alone; we live in God's world."

4. The concept of the human being as "steward" is one of the most provocative of biblical symbols for our time. See my book *The Steward: A Biblical Symbol Come of Age,* rev. ed. (Grand Rapids, Mich.: Wm. B. Eerdmans, 1990).

5. This Greek term is often translated as "suffering love," and that is acceptable as long as it is understood to mean a love that willingly takes on the suffering of "the other." The term certainly does not sanction masochism!

6. "The love of God does not find, but creates, that which is pleasing to it. The love of man comes into being through that which is pleasing to it. . . . the love of God . . . loves sinners, evil persons, fools, and weaklings in order to make them righteous, good, wise, and strong. Rather than seeking its own good, the love of God flows forth and bestows good. Therefore sinners are attractive because they are loved; they are not loved because they are attractive. . . . This is the love of the cross, born of the cross, which turns in the direction where it does not find good which it may enjoy, but where it may confer good on the bad and needy person . . . . . " (Martin Luther, *Luther's Works* [Philadelphia: Fortress Press, 1957], 31:57-58.

Chapter 6. Why Church? (And by the Way, What about "The Others"?)

1. Book 1 of Augustine's *Confessions*.

2. Strictly speaking, the Greek word *basileia* that older versions of the Bible translate as "kingdom" means "kingship" or "kingly rule, reign, or sovereignty." The nearness of God's reign was central to the message Jesus preached. He was not a utopian or a revolutionary exhorting people to build a "new world order"; rather, he invited and urged them to participate in the new life that *God* was creating in their midst (Luke 17:21) by accepting God's reign.

3. For example, a small, easily understood book entitled *The End of Christendom and the Future of Christianity* (Valley Forge, Pa.: Trinity Press International, 1997).

Chapter 7. Is There Any Hope?

1. These are all metaphors used by Jesus in the Sermon on the Mount (Matthew 5–7).

2. Paul Lehmann, *Ethics in a Christian Context* (New York: Harper & Row, 1963), 75ff.

Afterword

1. See Daniel Quinn, *Ishmael* (New York: Bantam/Turner Books, 1993).

2. Vol. 1: *Thinking the Faith* (1991 [1989]); vol. 2: *Professing the Faith* (1993); vol. 3: *Confessing the Faith* (1996), all published by Fortress Press of Minneapolis.